The Ultimate
Chief Petty Officer
Guidebook

James Glass

SB

Savas Beatie

California

Library of Congress Cataloging-in-Publication Data

Glass, James C.
The ultimate Chief Petty Officer guidebook : tips, tactics, and techniques for sailors who are serious about becoming a Chief Petty Officer / James C. Glass. — 1st edition.
pages cm
ISBN 978-1-61121-124-5
1. United States. Navy—Petty officers' handbooks. I. Title.
V123.G56 2013
359.00973—dc23
2013002735

SB

Published by
Savas Beatie LLC
989 Governor Drive, Suite 102
El Dorado Hills, CA 95762

Phone: 916-941-6896
(email) customerservice@savasbeatie.com

First edition, first printing
10 9 8 7 6 5 4 3 2

Savas Beatie titles are available at special discounts for bulk purchases in the United States by corporations, institutions, and other organizations. For more details, please contact Special Sales, P.O. Box 4527, El Dorado Hills, CA 95762, or you may e-mail us at sales@savasbeatie.com, or visit our website at www.savasbeatie.com for additional information.

Front cover: AGC (1DW/SW) Jose Morales

Proudly published, printed, and warehoused in the United States of America.

This book is dedicated to all
Chief Petty Officers. Past, present, and future.

And for my wife whose dedication to our family
made my dedication to the Navy possible.
Her unwavering faith inspires me every day.

Contents

Preface

My main purpose in writing this book is to help sailors achieve the goal of becoming a chief petty officer.

Beyond that, once they become chief petty officers themselves, helping the sailors who come along behind them is what chief petty officers do, and I want to make sure every new chief knows this. An E7 is someone who may be interested in helping only himself. But this book is about becoming a chief petty officer instead: someone who helps others achieve their goals.

This book is not about your test results coming back on your selection to E7; it's not about the transition from first class petty officer to chief petty officer; it's not about the induction season—because no book could ever capture the reality of that transition, and no book should be written about it. Besides, the transition is different for each chief who goes through it, and means something different to each chief.

Instead, this book is more about getting selected by the chief petty officer selection board. But actually becoming a chief involves more than being selected. It's about learning—especially, learning to be a leader. This includes leadership by example. No one wants a leader who doesn't set the example for others to follow. When I came into the Navy as a fireman recruit, I heard from some of my superiors, "Do as I say, not as I do." If this is you, maybe you should take a hard look in the mirror. Are you a leader, or do you just want to be in charge? Because there's a big difference between them—one that will be covered in this book.

If you feel you already possess all the intangibles for becoming a chief petty officer, I wish you all the best. However, if you need some assistance in preparing yourself to be a chief petty officer, you're not alone. Almost everyone needs assistance along the way.

Becoming a chief petty officer was a goal I set for myself and achieved during my U.S. Navy career. It took hard work, dedication, and focusing on the goals I set for myself—plus a lot of assistance from others—to be selected to chief petty officer. Then, after more than 22 years in the Navy and having achieved the rank of master chief petty officer, I decided to write this book. It became my focus to provide a tool other sailors could use to help them achieve their goal of becoming a chief petty officer, too. By combining my own experiences with information gathered from other chief petty officers, I believe I have put together a Chief Petty Officer Guidebook that will be a great tool for future chief petty officers.

This book provides sailors with an outline or road map. But just buying and reading it is not enough. Sailors must take action to get results. You must set goals—and then actually work hard to achieve them. In the end, doing so will pay huge dividends. If you don't do these things, then you're engaged in nothing more than wishful thinking—and I don't believe the chief petty officer selection board has ever selected anyone based on wishful thinking. Just because you want to become a chief petty officer doesn't mean it will happen. Hard work, dedication, and being a well-rounded sailor are just some of the attributes needed to become a chief petty officer.

Not everyone is cut out to be a chief petty officer. You need to take another look in the mirror to decide what path you want to take in your career. Maybe you prefer a path based on other choices, other goals. But if you waste an opportunity that would enhance your chances of advancement to chief petty officer, you may discover after the fact that it was your best, or even your only, chance to be selected. The direction of your career is your decision, and you need to think about it carefully.

One thing this book is not about: if your goal is not to become a chief petty officer but a limited duty officer (LDO), ask for a career development board to find out how to achieve this. I am not an LDO and never wanted to become one. In saying this I'm not disparaging your choice or try and alter your decision, because we need good officers in the wardroom—especially former enlisted sailors. Other sailors tell me they want to become a chief petty officer en route to becoming an LDO. If this is the route you want to follow, I applaud your decision—but don't make this the only path you pursue. The chief petty officer and LDO selection boards, while both very competitive, look at different criteria when determining the finest candidates. Don't make the mistake of wasting what may be your best opportunity to achieve your goal. Remember: you need to know what you want—don't let others decide for you.

I would like to see every sailor "succeed," however he or she defines it. Even for those whose goals do not include becoming a chief petty officer, *The Ultimate Chief Petty Officer Guidebook* can be a very useful tool on your professional journey. After all, one of the hardest things each of us is tasked with is "doing the right thing." We need to know what "the right thing" is if we are to do it, and each sailor needs to decide what the "right thing" is for him or her.

While I want every sailor to succeed at his or her goals, if your goal is to become a chief petty officer, you will need to set yourself apart from the rest of your peers. To do so, you need to use everything—including this book—to your advantage. That doesn't mean making your peers look bad; it means you need to prove to the chief petty officer selection board that you're the best candidate and should be selected. Either way, the record of your past actions will speak loud and clear to the selection board about what your goals are and how serious you are about achieving them. Ask yourself: what do my actions say about me?

Even if the board will select only one candidate, you need to ask yourself, "Have I set myself apart from my peers?" If the answer is yes, you're on the right track to being selected; if not, you have some work to do. But just because you have some work in front of you, don't get discouraged. You have the ability to change. Just focus: set your goals, and then work to achieve them. This reminds me of a saying I heard years ago: "Shoot for the moon—even if you miss, you'll be among the stars."

This guidance applies to everyone. We all need goals; the goal-setting process should never end. Even after I became a master chief petty officer, I had goals. One of my goals became to write this book—to assist you in achieving your goals of becoming a chief petty officer. In that way, it was written for you, not me. It's your career—and I hope this book will provide a foundation to build upon and the tools you need to reach your goals. Good luck on your journey.

Acknowledgments

My specific rating specialty within the Navy was in the surface community. I was an Interior Communications Electrician for the first thirteen years of my career, then a master-at-arms for the remainder. But in writing this book I gathered information from experts in other communities. I would like to thank all the people who helped make this book a reality—without their unwavering support it would not have been possible. All the chief petty officers from whom I received input in writing this book were essential to its success. Although I will mention only a few individuals within the chiefs' community by name, these shining examples are reflected in any chiefs' mess. They are all true leaders.

First I would like to thank Command Master Chief (CMDCM) Herbert Kelton. He challenged me to write *The Ultimate Chief Petty Officer Guidebook*. His expertise as a leader and mentor were instrumental to my own success as a sailor. His extensive knowledge as a master chief petty officer combined with his ability to motivate sailors exemplifies the foundation of any chiefs' mess, and I have learned so much from him. He is definitely "a sailors' sailor."

I would like to thank some who assisted me most within each community. These experts in their fields helped make sure *The Ultimate Chief Petty Officer Guidebook* represented a broad spectrum. I am very grateful for the insight and expertise provided by the submarine community's CMDCM Rafael Rosado and MTCS Timothy Hallwirth (my classmate at Grand Canyon University; thanks, brother). I also benefited from a wealth of knowledge and information from ABCM Jeffrey Jones and ABHC Eddie Padgett from the aviation community. Their insights were instrumental in writing this book; they are both true professionals within their communities and the Navy. I also received valuable information from BUCS John Maccallum from the Seabee community. He's one of the smartest Seabees I've ever had the pleasure to work with (we were both assigned to Naval Support Activity Lakehurst, New Jersey).

Although I am not an expert within these respective communities, I knew where I could get the information I needed. It was a great feeling to know I could always count on the chiefs' mess. It's a fraternity like no other.

The knowledge base and assistance of my fellow chiefs was invaluable in writing *The Ultimate Chief Petty Officer Guidebook*, and I thank each of them for helping me get it right. That's important, because the book isn't for me, it's for you. Its purpose is to get the best information out to all interested sailors, to benefit you in your careers, including by achieving the rank of chief petty officer.

Finally, I would like to thank my editor, Rob Ayer and publisher Ted Savas. Both believed in me and made sure I got it right. Without their dedication and support, *The Ultimate Chief Petty Officer Guidebook* would not have become a reality.

Chapter 1

Setting and Achieving Goals

The Importance of Goals

Do you wonder why the first class petty officer you work with was selected for chief and you weren't? I've heard many first class petty officers who were not selected say, "How did he get selected? I'm a better petty officer than he is."

The overall reason is this: the first class who was selected—like our example, YN1 (SW/AW) John Robbins—made it a *goal* to be a chief petty officer; whereas the other first class petty officer—like our YN1 (SW) Gary Allen—made it a "hope" that the board would select him to chief. (See the Introduction for first mention of our example first class petty officers, and also the separate section on them later in this chapter.)

One of the subsidiary reasons YN1 Robbins was selected to chief is because he was competitive among his peers and consistently—year after year—ranked above the senior rater's average on evaluations; whereas YN1 Allen, who was not selected, while also consistently ranked above the senior rater's average on evaluations, believes that being an expert in his field is the only thing the chief petty officer selection board looks for.

Was this the deciding factor on why Petty Officer Robbins was selected to chief petty officer and Petty Officer Allen was not? If not, what were some of the other factors? Throughout the book we'll look at each of these two sailors and compare their careers against each other's. We'll study their goals and what they've achieved. By the end of the book, you'll understand why Petty Officer Robbins was selected to chief petty officer while Petty Officer Allen was not. Let me remind you that both of these sailors are great at their jobs, as recognized by their respective commands. However, you'll clearly see who is the better, more *well-rounded* sailor overall. *To be selected to be a chief petty officer, you must be a well-rounded sailor.*

You've probably seen many changes so far in your career. By this point it should be obvious that simply doing your job is no longer enough—if it ever was—to get you selected by the chief petty officer selection board. Those of you who have been board-eligible time and time again may actually see this pattern better than your peers who've already been selected. Those already selected have been busy. They've been doing more than just their jobs, which has made them competitive among their peers, standing out among their contemporaries. Being the best at your job is good—but it's not enough. You must clearly show the selection board why you're the one who should be selected ahead of your peers. This will make you more "marketable," so to speak, before the selection board.

If you've never set goals for yourself, you're hurting your chances for success at any level. Goal-setting is the way to see results from your hard work. If, instead, you are just "spit-balling" it—merely hoping that things will work out or fall into place, simply because you want them to—instead of actually setting goals for yourself to achieve, then you need to speak to your chiefs. Ask if any of them were just "hoping" to become a chief petty officer. I doubt you'll find even one. Remember the old saying: "Hope is not a strategy."

Becoming a chief petty officer will take hard work on your part. This includes planning ahead and setting goals; otherwise you'll never achieve them. If you're already able to do this, you're well on your way to success. However, if you find this difficult, ask for a career development board. Career development boards can help you put goals in place that you can achieve. Instead of just hoping you're doing the right things and then letting the chips fall where they may, you'll have more confidence in your approach. Similarly, you may be working hard at achieving goals right now, but are they the right goals? Your chief can play a pivotal role in helping you answer this question. The confidence you gain from consultations with career development boards and your chiefs will help you set and achieve even more goals in the future.

The Right Goals

The goals you set for yourself need to be realistic, and you must have a vision in place for achieving them. "Realistic" means goals you can actually achieve. For example, earning an associate's degree within the next two years is a realistic goal, whereas earning a doctorate within the next two years, when you haven't yet earned your associate's degree, is not achievable. Starting with earning an associate's degree will help you achieve the next goal, which should be a bachelor's degree. A sailor who envisions earning his doctorate can achieve this only through setting and achieving other, necessary, intermediate goals along the way. Failure to do so sets the sailor up for failure, not success. This is true in an overall fashion for any sailor who wants to be a chief petty officer: achieving this large goal requires setting and achieving many smaller goals along the way.

The Wheel of Success should provide you with achievable goals. It is a sort of roadmap for determining a path to success. Those of us who use electronic gadgets instead of a map can often find ourselves taking a wrong turn, and sometimes it can be difficult to get back on track, especially when the electronic gadget is recalculating just at the moment we need to make a decision: do I go right or left?

You will need to make many decisions, about a lot of areas. After all, the chief petty officer selection board is looking for a well-rounded sailor, not the sailor who is just the best technician, administrator, or logistician. Although being the best at your field of work is good, to be competitive you must take on those additional duties that will break you out from among your peers. Think about it: if you're before the chief petty officer selection board, you're probably the best in your field; but the other candidates are likely to be, too. If everyone is the best *in his or her field*, then what separates the best *overall* candidates, those who'll be selected by the board? Being well-rounded sailors.

You need to become more competitive among your peers, and you need to learn how to do this. A good mentor will tell you when things are going well, but should also tell you when you need to step it up by setting new, more challenging goals. As mentioned previously, your chief and/or a career development board can play an integral part in advancing your career. You don't have to go at it alone when it comes to your career. Don't be the sailor who already knows everything, yet has not been selected by the chief petty officer selection board for several years. Instead of trying to be a "sea lawyer," get the right answers. Be right, not wrong.

Introducing Our Petty Officers

As we go through each chapter of this book, we'll compare our two example first class petty officers with each other. This includes looking at their approaches to setting and achieving goals, and how those approaches will play in front of the chief petty officer selection board. Did one of the petty officers set realistic goals, while the other did not? Did one man's goals align with what the selection board was looking for, while the other's did not? Again: a career development board and conversations with your chief or mentor can help you know the answers to these questions ahead of time.

Petty Officer Robbins

- He's the leading petty officer in the Administration Department (Shore Duty) at Personnel Support Detachment, Norfolk, Virginia.

- He's been in the Navy for 10 years, and will be taking the chief petty officer exam for the first time.

- He works well with others. As president of the First Class Petty Officer Association, he provides in-depth advancement training for all sailors at the second class petty officer level and below. He also conducts advancement games, such as "Advancement Jeopardy" and "Stump the Chief," which not only help sailors gain more knowledge about their rating and the Navy but also build camaraderie within the command.

- As the command funeral and honors detail coordinator, he's coordinated more than 200 funeral honors and 20 color guard ceremonies.

- He was selected as the senior Sailor of the Quarter and is preparing for the Sailor of the Year board, to be held in a few months.

- He completed a Global War on Terror Support Assignment tour in Iraq for 379 days and received a Joint Service Commendation Medal.

- Previously he had a reporting career development board; another one after being on board for six months; and one after being on board for 12 months, as well. But it's been more than a year since, so he's requested a career development board to find out where he stands in relation to his current goals and how they align with what the upcoming chief petty officer selection board will most likely use as criteria to select the best candidates.

This career development board will be comprised of Robbins' chain of command, along with the command master chief and command career counselor. The following personnel will be present:

- CMDCM (SW/EXW) Gulbranson, Command Master Chief

- YNCM (SW/AW) Lawrence, Admin Officer

- YNC (SW/SCW) McCoy, Admin Leading Chief Petty Officer

- NCC (SW) Garrison, Command Career Counselor

The goals Robbins has set for himself are listed below. Are they realistic? If he not only sets but achieves his short-term goals, will this make him more likely to be selected by the board (one of his long-term goals)? Do you share some of his goals?

Robbins' Goals:
(Short term—one year or less)

1. Within three months, complete bachelor's degree (has only two more classes to complete)

2. On the next command physical fitness assessment, receive an overall Low Outstanding or better

3. Earn Military Outstanding Volunteer Service Medal (in two months will have more than three years of community service)

4. Be selected as Sailor of the Year

Robbins' Goals:
(Long term—more than one year)

1. Be selected as a chief petty officer

2. Complete master's degree

3. Pay off credit cards and be debt-free

Petty Officer Allen

- He is the Leading Petty Officer in the Administration Department (Sea Duty) on board the USS *Mobile Bay* (CG 53).

- He's been in the Navy for 16 years, and this will be his fourth time taking the chief petty officer exam. He's been chief petty officer board-eligible each time.

- He's a very talented and knowledgeable yeoman. Anytime a chief or officer comes into the Admin Office, he makes sure he takes care of their questions or concerns right away.

- He is starting to learn how to delegate his duties to the junior sailors in the Administration Office.

- He requires his sailors to study 2.5 hours a week in the office to prepare them for their upcoming advancement exams; he also ensures they complete at least one Navy Knowledge Online course each Friday before they go home.

- He has never been Sailor of the Quarter or Sailor of the Year; he feels politics are the key to being selected as either.

- He's been on board the *Mobile Bay* for three years and is negotiating for orders. He's decided he wants shore duty in Japan; his ship is homeported in Japan, and he was previously stationed at Personnel Support Detachment Yokosuka, Japan.

- From Yokosuka he completed a 179-day Individual Augmentee assignment in Kuwait. He did not receive any awards during this assignment—likely because his focus was on getting back home, not competing among his peers. Although he was not recognized with an award, he feels he has "checked the box" by volunteering for the Individual Augmentee assignment.

- When he transfers soon, the command's awards board has decided he will receive an end-of-tour award: his third Navy Achievement Medal. It will be the only award he's received from the command during his three-year assignment.

- He knows the chief petty officer exam will be coming up again in January, and has started studying for the exam. He's been board-eligible each of the three previous times, and he feels this is his best opportunity to be selected.

- He has not had a career development board since the one-year point at this command, almost two years ago. While he's never said so to any of the chiefs, he believes he already knows what the selection board will be looking for; after all, he's been board-eligible before.

Petty Officer Allen will be meeting with YNC (AW) Geraldine, the Leading Chief Petty Officer for the Admin Department. He wants Chief Geraldine to look at his chief petty officer board package. Allen's package had 21 enclosures last year, and he would like to increase that this year. He feels that to be selected to chief, it's necessary to overload the selection board with all of his previous achievements, so that's his goal. In contrast, YNC Geraldine told Petty Officer Allen that his package had too many enclosures last year, and that he should update them into his electronic service record.

Your Record

If this description of Allen—especially the last part—sounds like you, you need to speak to your chiefs. More is not always better! Some first class petty officers figure that if they send in to the board their entire career—every evaluation, every page four, every award—they're better off. But most selection board members only want enclosures sent if something is missing from your official military record. Not everything in your record needs to be submitted. For example, if you were merely nominated as

Sailor of the Quarter, and submitted this nomination to the board, I doubt the members would even notice. If you want clarification on what should and should not be submitted, speak to the chiefs at your command (I recommend you get at least two to look at your package for any errors or updates) and/or request a career development board to review it.

If these reviews of your record turn up missing items, forward them via your administration office to the Naval Personnel Command to be entered into your official military record. (An example cover letter is available on the NPC website.) The chief petty officer selection board will want to know whether you've been updating your record or are just hoping everything is correct. The future of your career depends on your record, so you should know what's in it. Perhaps someone else's information, such as a report of a nonjudicial punishment or an award, got into your record by mistake. If you're not serious about keeping track of what's in your record, why should the selection board take you seriously?

Chapter 2

Are You a Leader?

"Leaders aren't born, they're made. And they're made just like anything else, through hard work. And that's the price we'll have to pay to achieve that goal, or any goal."

–Vince Lombardi

Leadership and Management

Are you a leader or a manager?

First of all, what's the difference between the two? Does a leader have to lead people? Does a manager have to be in charge of people? What really is the difference?

A leader doesn't have to be in charge of people to be a leader. A leader can be anyone who inspires people to do their best. Leaders have followers. Managers, on the other hand, tell people what to do. Managers have subordinates working for them.

Can leaders have subordinates? Yes. Sometimes leaders are also managers: they have subordinates working for them because they're in supervisory positions. But they lead their subordinates by example, and they inspire their people to do their best.

Conversely, great managers may have leaders working for them, which allows them to delegate.

No one is born a great leader, just as no one is born an effective manager. Although every person possesses the potential to become a great leader, manager, or both, the necessary characteristics are learned traits, not engrained in our DNA.

TABLE 1: A Leader vs. A Manager

Although the list is not all-inclusive, this table summarizes some of the differences between a leader and a manager.

SUBJECT	LEADER	MANAGER
Fundamental nature	Change	Constant
Focus	Inspiring people	Managing work
Encompasses	Followers	Subordinates
Goals	Long-term	Short-term
Seeks	Vision	Objectives
Approach	Sets direction	Plans in detail
Decisions	Facilitates	Makes
Power	Charismatic personality	Formal authority
Insists on	Heart	Head
Instills energy thru	Passion	Control
Diversity	Forms	Endorses
Measures used	Proactive	Reactive
Influence	Sell	Tell
Style of approach	Transformational	Transactional
Exchange	Excited for work	Money for work
Likes	Striving for excellence	Action
Wants	Achievement/Teamwork	Results
Conflict	Uses	Avoids
Direction	New ideas	Stay on the path
Truth	Seeks	Creates
Concern	What is right	Being right
Credit	Gives	Takes
Blame	Accepts	Assigns
Decision making skills	Will make hard decisions	Looks for the easy way out

Control

If you want to change your identity from manager to leader, you must learn to give up some of your authority, or at least some of your control. A leader has to be willing to relinquish some power so that a follower can be assigned a task, take the lead, and see it through from start to finish. When leaders inspire someone else to do a job, the product usually turns out better than the leader expected. In contrast, when managers assign a task to their subordinates, they usually impose tight constraints, from start to finish, on how the job is to be completed. The result may be exactly what the manager was looking for: nothing less—and nothing more—than expected.

When I became a chief petty officer, I learned to delegate some of my duties to the first and second class petty officers who worked for me. I felt this gave them the opportunity to shine. But then I learned an even better way to lead my sailors: the art of empowerment. Full coverage of the subject of empowerment is beyond the scope of this book, but here's a brief discussion. I had never heard of the term before I became a chief petty officer. My command master chief at the time, CMDCM (AW/SW) Holman, taught me what the term meant and how to use it to get the most out of my sailors—advice I greatly appreciated. I began to toy with the idea of empowerment, and after I learned what it could do, I really wanted to use it. Empowerment became another great tool for me as a leader.

However, there are some downsides to empowerment. Some sailors are not ready to take on the responsibility involved, so they may crash and burn—and possibly take you down with them. (In such cases, training is essential to the success of empowerment.) As a leader, I was ready to take the chance of things possibly going the wrong way, and was ready to take the responsibility if they did. Too many people in supervisory roles blame someone else when failures occur, instead of taking responsibility for their decisions as leaders and managers. Being a leader isn't just a matter of being there to take credit when things go right; a leader accepts the blame when things go wrong as well, because a leader knows there will be successes as well as failures.

I've also learned that, while empowerment is a great tool, some supervisors don't want to give up their control. That's because they're afraid of two things. One is that things could go wrong, which will make them look bad in front of their subordinates and supervisors. The other thing they fear is that the person they empower will do such a great job they'll look bad by comparison. Great leaders, including great chief petty officers, know this should not be the issue. As chief petty officers, we're in the business of building up leaders, not suppressing them. If you're going to "throw someone under the bus" (make someone else look bad in order to make yourself look good), maybe you should become a Limited Duty Officer. (Just kidding—that's an old chiefs' joke.) One reason you won't succeed that way is because chiefs are not ignorant. Although you may think you're pulling a fast one on them, they'll know what's going on. This is not just because chiefs have eyes in the backs of their heads (which they do), but because, plainly put, people talk, and they love to inform the chiefs about why things went wrong.

Bad Leadership

A leader's ability to react, adapt, and overcome depends on his or her leadership skills. I've made many mistakes as a leader, but during my Navy career I also had some great successes. I learned valuable lessons through my own failures, and I tried not to make the same mistake twice. And I learned from the failures of other leaders, bad as well as good.

Are there bad leaders? Of course. We've all seen examples of bad leaders, and have probably worked for at least one during our careers. Mostly I learned from them what *not* to do.

Micromanagers

Many people are put off by the word "micromanagement" because the connotations are so negative. But micromanagement is a tool, and it can be used in a positive or negative way. It can get things accomplished; you yourself may use micromanagement to get things done.

But if those in power use only this style of management, working for them may seem like a game of survival. Often supervisors practice micromanagement to show subordinates they have all the power. Some micromanagers exercise their power just because they love to and because they can. They control how the work gets done—monitoring it from start to finish—then decide whether the product meets their approval.

Instead, the best use of micromanagement is to get everyone working on the same mission, toward a common goal. When this has been accomplished, a true leader relinquishes the reins, perhaps to a micromanager, either through delegation or empowerment. He then shifts to another style of leadership.

Narcissists

Narcissistic leaders truly believe it's all about them—that they are the center of the universe. They take criticism, or even any sort of disagreement, personally, and consider it akin to mutiny. To narcissists, you're either with them or against them, and only those who are with them are admitted to the inner circle, where all the favors and plum assignments are doled out.

When I was stationed aboard the USS *Thomas S. Gates*, my commanding officer was a narcissistic leader. I came across this type of leader again at the end of my career when I was the command master chief at Naval Weapons Station Earle. Even worse, at Earle, not only was the commanding officer a narcissist, he also couldn't make an informed decision—something every leader must be able to expect from his subordinates. A leader who can't make decisions only hurts those under him who can.

Leaders and Subordinates

As a leader, I can always learn more. A good leader accepts constructive criticism, learns from his mistakes, and moves on. I expect those around me to be able to make a decision—right, wrong, or indifferent—and, if it's the wrong one, to learn from it.

To be successful, leaders must have the support and be able to use the knowledge of their subordinates. Leaders will never have all the answers to begin with, but if they draw on the people around them and network with others beyond that, they'll find the answers. Leaders who see themselves as highly successful, who feel they already have all the answers, often lack faith in their subordinates. But subordinates want to succeed too, and they need leadership, guidance, and mentoring to do so. It's an unsuccessful leader who treats subordinates with disdain and a lack of trust, or fails to create a climate in which they feel free to express their feelings and offer their ideas.

Leaders need to be able to pull the best from people, but not every subordinate can be led the same way, so leading them all may take some ingenuity on your part. Having many different management and leadership styles available to you will only make you a better leader and manager. However, while different leadership theories can be learned in the classroom, they must be practiced in the workplace. Becoming a good leader is an ongoing process. To be even more successful in the future, you need to draw on what has worked for you in the past and from your other personal experiences.

As a first class petty officer, you've probably been somewhat successful to this point. Always remember those who provided you the positive leadership and mentoring that enabled your success. Pay this benefit forward by affording your sailors the same opportunities through your effective leadership. Sailors will replicate what they see in their leaders, so it's imperative to share what we've learned so it will be passed on to the next generation. You shouldn't take this too far, however. When you find a good leader who sets the right example, it's okay to learn from him or her, but don't try to make yourself a clone. Use their talents to your advantage, but you are your own person, so be yourself.

Leadership must apply to the area of personal development as well. We cannot become so engrossed in our professional careers that we forget about our responsibilities regarding personal growth. How many times have we seen a sailor who's outstanding at work get a DUI, be involved in a domestic dispute, or pay no child support for months? Financial problems in a sailor's personal life can cause him to lose the security clearance he needs to do his job. A good leader knows when to use intrusive leadership with his sailors to make sure they don't make the wrong decisions in their off-duty lives, or simply become too complacent. A great leader is available 24 hours a day, including weekends and holidays.

Models and Lessons

It took many years for me to become the leader I am today. After all those years of learning positive things from others as well as from my own and others' mistakes, I believe I am a very good leader. Although I don't know everything, I know where to go when I need assistance. The chief's mess in general has long been a repository for a wealth of knowledge, and being able to draw on it when I needed helped me immensely.

Two leaders in particular who had a role in my success are John Lippolis and Gary Hastings. John and Gary were both retired master chief petty officers with whom I was fortunate to be stationed in the Security Department at Naval Air Station Brunswick, Maine. John was the operations commander and Gary was the security director; at the time I was the deputy security officer and the leading chief petty officer.

John impressed on me the importance of taking care of my sailors, and he also mentored me on my career path. Although John had been retired from the Navy for about ten years at the time, he was still able to give me sound advice on my career. His advice was invaluable and was pivotal in my being selected as a senior chief petty officer and master chief petty officer. He provided me with a path, a visual roadmap, and helped me set and achieve goals along the way. Having this tool was instrumental in my success, both as a leader and in achieving rank. Sadly, John passed away in 2011. He will be missed by many sailors, friends, and colleagues who knew him throughout his many years. I'm proud he was my friend.

Gary Hastings showed me that as a leader you don't need to have all the answers, just know where to get them. Gary was successful because he not only preached this philosophy, he acted on it. He surrounded himself with people who would be able to make informed decisions within the department, such as the deputy security director, operations commander, training officer, and physical security specialist. Gary taught me another tool I've used many times in my career and since retiring: empowerment (mentioned earlier in this chapter). He taught me that empowering your people gives them the opportunity to lead instead of just follow. Empowerment allows sailors to become leaders themselves, under your mentorship. There is no greater satisfaction than seeing others succeed. Having great leaders like John Lippolis and Gary Hastings to learn from gave me the capacity as a leader to empower others and teach them what I had learned, through both successes and failures.

I joined the Navy shortly after graduating from high school, and learned many things from the Navy by the time I retired. These included integrity, leadership, mentorship, and, above all, doing the right thing. Doing the right thing is easier said than done. I haven't always done the right thing—this was a weakness of mine. How many of us have done the right thing all the time?

Here are some examples of what I'm talking about. Were you ever at the commissary or exchange, or even at your own command, when you saw a sailor wearing an unsat uniform: shirt not fully tucked in, gig line off-center, or no cover? Perhaps this sailor was wearing organizational clothing with a uniform when not authorized. What did you do? On paper or in the classroom, we know what we should do, and we can tell others; but when we see it happening in the real world, do we do the right thing? Would you approach the sailor and tell him to square away? What if this sailor was an officer; would you still do the right thing? If you do the right thing by letting that officer know what's wrong with his uniform, he may thank you afterwards, because he may have been unaware of the problem.

I didn't always do the right thing. Now I do, because I learned that doing the right thing includes doing so all the time. When I was stationed aboard the USS *Monterey* (CG 61) (then homeported in Mayport, Florida) we had a visit from the chief of naval operations. Admiral Boorda, on one of his many tours, spoke to several thousand sailors from around the base, first updating them on all sorts of issues, then answering questions. During this particular visit he spoke about doing the right thing, and I took particular notice of his admonition: "Do the right thing—twice when no one is looking." Although this quote may not have hit everyone the way it did me that day, I took it to heart. It made me want to become a better sailor. Ever since that day I've worked on doing the right thing, and it has made me a better leader. Good leadership includes leading by example. I learned that when I did the right thing in front of sailors, it became easier for them to do the same.

After retiring from the Navy, I got a job as a site security manager at Naval Air Station Whiting Field. Retiring from the Navy scared me a little due to the transition to a civilian workforce. So I spoke to several chiefs who had made the transition before me, and what I learned from their experiences was very helpful. I gained new goals to set and achieve. This, combined with the knowledge and experience from my Navy career, made me very successful in my new role. This is yet another example of how the knowledge I gained from the chiefs' mess helped me become a better leader, not only in the Navy but after retiring. Great leaders are needed in every aspect of every job, both in and out of the Navy. Leaders have the ability to lead anywhere they're needed. Being a great leader is something you'll be able to use whatever you do.

In the chiefs' mess there's a saying: "Take care of your sailors, and they'll take care of you." A great leader in the Navy tends to be a sailors' sailor. Because such leaders take care of their sailors, and their sailors know it, they'll do anything to support their leaders. They excel *for their leaders*. Sometimes when this happens, we as leaders need to pull back on the reins a little. Because no one else will step up to the challenge, outstanding petty officers sometimes take on the whole load of command, collateral, and additional duties—to the point where they crash and burn. (I discuss this further in Chapter VII.) When we see this happening, it's imperative we speak to the other first class petty officers about responsibility—including taking on more of it. Doing just "your job" isn't enough, and if we as leaders allow our sailors to think it is, we're not setting them up for success.

In the Navy and in life, there's plenty of work to do, and few enough to do it. We all need to put our shoulders to the wheel.

There's more to being a leader than always being in charge; a leader can set the example even when he's not. Leading is sometimes about following: to be able to lead, you also must be able to follow others. This is a lesson all chiefs learn, and I myself have passed it on to many other chiefs. If you can't follow others, you'll never be a chief petty officer. You may be an E7, but I doubt you'd like to be addressed by this title, and I doubt it's how you'd like to be remembered.

Two people worth mentioning on leadership and goal-setting toward becoming a chief petty officer are ABHC (AW/SW) (retired) Val Stevens and Command Master Chief Rafael Rosado. They're both great sailors who have great stories about the road to becoming a chief petty officer. They set great examples of taking care of their sailors and following as well as leading, and they had a very positive impact on me.

I met Chief Petty Officer Stevens after I retired from the Navy. My first post-Navy job was for Securiguard, Inc., as a site security manager. I had approximately 60 outstanding security guards working for me, one of whom was Val Stevens.

Val Scott Stevens enlisted in the Navy in 1985 under the buddy program. When he headed off to boot camp, he immediately had a bad feeling; boot camp sets a bad tone for most sailors. But for Stevens, like so many sailors before him, the feeling soon subsided. During boot camp Stevens had his first encounter with a chief, his company commander. He found out the chief was a stickler for the rules, making boot camp even more difficult. This encounter during boot camp showed Airman Stevens how much power a chief petty officer can have. He hadn't yet made a decision on whether to stay in the Navy for the long haul, but he knew that if he did he wanted to become a chief petty officer himself.

After boot camp Stevens went to the USS *Constellation* (CV-64). His chief saw the potential in the young airman; they became mentor and protégé. Stevens listened to the advice of his chief petty officer, and advanced to third class petty officer. This advice also was vital in helping him learn his rating as an aviation boatswain's mate, which directly resulted in his advancing to second class petty officer.

Newly frocked ABHC (AW/SW) Val Scott Stevens, left) standing next to his brother, Lt. Mark Stevens.

Val Stevens

When Petty Officer Stevens was stationed at Naval Air Facility, Misawa, Japan, he met ABHCS Wingerter and ABFC Mendoza. While at Misawa, these two mentors taught him a lot more about his rating, and also about becoming a well-rounded sailor. This confirmed for him that he wanted to become a chief petty officer, like his mentors. And it was just a few years later Petty Officer Stevens did just that. By setting goals for himself and achieving them through hard work and dedication, he was selected to chief petty officer.

Just like his own mentors did with him, Chief Petty Officer Stevens kept helping sailors. When a second class petty officer got in some trouble with police in a different state, Chief Stevens drove to the police station and spoke to the police officer. After some conversation, he asked the police officer to turn the young sailor over to him, and guaranteed the sailor would not be back. The police officer released the sailor. This sailor had never had a mentor; now Chief Stevens took him under his wing, just as his mentors had done for him earlier in his career. He put his time into developing this sailor—who eventually was selected to chief petty officer, and recently master chief petty officer. Although Chief Stevens has retired from the Navy, he still helps sailors.

The second sailor I would like to recognize is Rafael Rosado, the command master chief for Naval Air Station Whiting Field in Milton, Florida. Master Chief Rosado is a very unusual sailor—and I say this with the highest regard. When he enlisted in the Navy 27 years ago, he set goals for himself almost immediately after completing boot camp. He was assigned to submarines and

Chief Petty Officer Stevens with his wife. Like so many successful Sailors, having a supportive spouse is one of the biggest reasons for their success.

Val Stevens

immediately began his journey toward becoming a chief petty officer. Working under the tutelage and guidance of his superiors, he set off on a course that resulted in his being selected as a chief petty officer in six and a half years. That's right: six and a half years. This feat is rarely achieved in the Navy. Even more impressively, Chief Rosado didn't stop setting goals at that point; instead he set a new standard for himself, and was selected to master chief petty officer after only 14 years of service. Again, this is not a typo. By setting his goals and working toward them, he achieved what only one percent of those in the Navy accomplish—reaching the rank of master chief petty officer. And doing so in only 14 years is amazing.

By setting and achieving goals, each of these outstanding sailors achieved his goal of becoming a chief petty officer. But remember, it wasn't just *setting* the goals that got them there; it was *achieving* them. Although we all fail to achieve some of our goals from time to time, the key is to rebound by re-setting existing goals or setting new ones, and achieving those.

Leading Yourself

When it comes down to it, the only person holding you back is you. If you want to, you can always find an excuse: "My chief isn't supportive;" "My command looks to people besides me to get things done," etc. Some of these factors may even be true. But ultimately it's up to you to set and achieve your goals. Otherwise all you're doing is wasting time—and possibly your career. If that's the approach you take, not only will you not be competitive among your peers for advancement, you may even be asked to leave the Navy.

Chapter 3

Evaluations

Evaluation Levels

Every enlisted sailor receives an evaluation annually. It's very important to know how these evaluations can help you be competitive among your peers. The chief petty officer selection board can go back as far as five years to review your evaluations and decide whether you're a star, average, or substandard performer. This means the chief petty officer selection board might look at evaluations you received as a second class petty officer. Receiving "sustained superior performance" evaluations along with being a well-rounded sailor will increase your chances of making a favorable impression. Some sailors suffer from the misconception that being a good sailor, well-liked, or the best at their job will, by itself, gain them a competitive evaluation.

Some raters do let their feelings dictate the rankings they assign in evaluations. We've all heard about "the good 'ol boy network." Some sailors get the best evaluations because they're close to their chiefs and are obedient to them, instead of receiving evaluations that reflect all aspects of their performance. When this dynamic is in effect in any command, department, or division, it quickly destroys morale.

Leaders must be able to differentiate between a good sailor and a great sailor. You and your peers are all running the same race; what do you need to do to set yourself apart from them? The truly stellar performer is the sailor who continually improves himself, is not afraid to take on hard assignments, furthers his education, and sets the example for others to emulate. He or she continually sets and achieves goals.

But be careful about the goals you set with regard to evaluations; don't be overly concerned with being an "early promote" sailor. You don't need to receive an "early promote" on every evaluation to be selected to chief petty officer. Ask your chiefs whether they had an "early promote" on every one of their evaluations. I'll predict that more than a few will tell you they were selected to chief despite receiving "must promote" or even "promotable" on some evaluations. They would probably go on to tell you that if they did receive a "promotable" evaluation, they soon improved to "must promote" or "early promote." They made up their minds to transition from being a good sailor to a great sailor.

There's a big difference between *wanting to* be an "early promote" sailor and actually *being* an "early promote" sailor. When I was selected to chief, to senior chief, and to master chief, my last five evaluations in each case were two "must promotes" and three "early promotes;" and for chief, one of the "early promotes" was a one-of-one. So, just because you have an evaluation lower than "early promote," don't be concerned. Some first class petty officers who have five or more "early promote" evaluations to show the selection board are not selected to chief petty officer. They probably figured their job performance alone would get them selected, so they didn't take on the additional responsibilities that would have made them more competitive among their peers.

What should concern you about your evaluation is the information it contains and how well it is written. For instance, if you're assuming additional command collateral duties, doing some community service, taking college courses or have earned a degree, and doing similar things that will set you apart from your peers, you're setting yourself up for success. However, if you receive "early promotes" yet take on none of the additional roles listed above, then you're not setting yourself up for success, even if you're the best technician, administrator, or logistician. If you try, you can probably think of first class petty officers who've been passed by their junior sailors who were more well-rounded.

Are you one of these sailors who's been passed by? If so, speak to your chief or ask for a career development board. Both these steps can help you set the goals necessary to become a chief petty officer. I'm not saying you shouldn't strive to earn "early promote" evaluations, but they won't guarantee you'll be selected to chief. If you stand out among your peers, the selection board will see this and you'll have a better chance than your contemporaries of being selected. If you don't take these steps, don't be surprised to see others continue to pass you by. You need to be the driving force behind your career, because no one else will be.

Reporters

The reporting senior's average plays a key role at the chief petty officer selection board, so it's important for you to know and understand this information. It tells the selection board whether you're below, at , or above the reporting senior's average. If you're below or at the reporting senior's average, you need to find out what you can do to make yourself more competitive.

However, I wouldn't get too worked up over this as long as you're moving up. For example, say you arrive at a new command, five months later the first class petty officer evaluations come out, and you receive a "promotable" evaluation. Don't panic. However, you may want to look back at your last command, remind yourself of what your evaluations were, determine how you stacked up against the other first class petty officers there, check what your senior rater's average was, and find out where you ranked. If for your three years you received three "promotable" evaluations there as well, you may want to start to panic. It probably means you didn't take on the additional duties that contribute to becoming a chief petty officer. If you did receive three consecutive "promotable" evaluations there, ask your current chiefs to help you figure out why, and what you need to do to become competitive at this command.

This would be a good time for reflection, for taking a hard, honest look at yourself and what you've done in your career to this point. If you feel you're being punished or singled out, take this to your chiefs' mess and listen to what they have to say. Be prepared: you may not like what you hear. But being able to take constructive criticism is crucial—and sometimes criticism is warranted. Listen to what the chiefs say and use it to become better. If you unjustly blame your last command for not giving you what you deserved on an evaluation, award, or anything else, take that long, hard look in the mirror, have someone kick you in the butt, and use it as a reality check. More than likely you received what you deserved. (However, if you genuinely feel you were singled out, meet with the Command Managed and Equal Opportunity Program Coordinator and find out. If you are indeed being singled out, you have rights.)

To find out where you really stand, take a close look at your record. If you had one "promotable," one "must promote," and an "early promote" during the three years at your last unit, that shows progression. Even if you received one "promotable" and two "must promote" evaluations, but the last "must promote" was higher than the previous "must promote" for the same reporting senior's average, you're still showing progression—and progression is the key to success.

The Whole Picture

Your evaluations should reflect your abilities in all ten areas represented on the Wheel of Success. (This will be discussed in greater detail beginning in Chapter 5.)

To help you determine what you need to accomplish to make yourself more competitive among your peers, ask for a career development board. Your chain of command, command master chief, career counselor, and you will take stock of where you are in your career. The board may find that you need to focus more on collateral duties, watch qualifications, duty stations, education, or leadership qualities.

An example of the latter would be to set a goal that every first class petty officer should: to be a leading petty officer. Leading other sailors well is the best way to show the chief petty officer selection board that you're ready to assume greater responsibilities. Being a leading petty officer isn't the only thing the selection board looks for—but it's one of the best markers. (For more on this subject, see Chapter 14.)

Boards look at your record with a very discerning eye. You may be a member of a certain organization, e.g., the First Class Petty Officer Association; you may even hold an office, such as president, vice president, treasurer, or secretary. But if you're not active, the board will be able to tell. If you are active in the association, record your actions in block 43 of the evaluation. However, if all you do is list your membership and other collateral duties in block 29, you're just wasting your time, because being inactive in a collateral duty is the same as not holding that responsibility at all. Work to your full potential! (See more on this subject in Chapter 8 as well.)

Evaluations and Mentors

I was lucky enough to have some great leaders mentor me during my naval career. MACM (SW) Jerome Carrubba was the first—when I'd already spent nine years in the Navy. Previously, many sailors had been my supervisors, leading petty officers, and chief petty officers, but none had ever taken the time to teach me the things I needed to know to become a leader and future mentor myself. At the time I met Chief Carrubba, I was an IC1 (SW) and he was chief master-at-arms on our ship, the USS *Thomas S. Gates* (CG-51), homeported at Naval Station Pascagoula, Mississippi. I became a duty master-at-arms as a collateral duty, and MACM Carrubba saw a lot of potential in me. As I became more and more involved with the master-at-arms rating, he saw the potential for me to become a great master-at-arms. I asked for a career development board.

Just at that time, MACM Carrubba got hurt and was transported off the ship. He recommended to the commanding officer that I take over the duties of chief master-at-arms, and the C.O. agreed. Because of my ability to shine as a duty master-at-arms, because of the potential Chief Carrubba saw in me, and because of the impact I made as chief master-at-arms, I was able to cross-rate over to master-at-arms. Based on my evaluations as chief master-at-arms, I was selected as Sailor of the Year on the *Gates*. What I learned through MACM Carrubba's mentorship, along with the great evaluations he wrote, made a direct contribution to my selection as a chief petty officer. Although I had many other mentors in my Navy career, MACM Carrubba was the first. He was one of those who taught me that taking care of your sailors is the most important role you can fulfill in a career in the Navy—without our sailors, we're out of a job.

I'm not saying that having a mentor will get you selected as a chief, but a great mentor can guide you in making sound decisions that will set you on a course to success.

Robbins and Allen: Two Evaluations

How do the evaluations on our two first class petty officers stack up against each other? We'll look at only the most recent evaluation for each—YN1 (SW) Allen's first, then YN1 (SW/EXW) Robbins'—plus the last five performance traits from their Performance Summary Records. Instead of looking at the entire evaluation, we'll focus on some key blocks. As you look at the evaluations of these two first class petty officers, focus on the write-ups, especially the attributes described. Then look at their Performance Summary Records to see what they've done—and both have done some great things over the past five years. But I hope you'll see that one has outperformed the other, and that there are good reasons one was selected to chief petty officer while the other was not.

Performance Reviews

YN1 (SW) Allen's most recent evaluation

---

29. Primary/Collateral/Watchstanding duties (Enter primary duty abbreviations in box.)

ADMIN LPO

PRI: Military Administration/Command and Staff LPO-12. Supervised 9 personnel in support of pay and personnel for 330 officers and enlisted Sailors. COLL: MDMAA-4, ***CMD Command Diversity Coordinator-12, FCPOA President-9.** WATCH: OOD Inport-12, CSOOW-6

---

43. COMMENTS ON PERFORMANCE. *All 1.0 marks, three 2.0 marks, and 2.0 marks in Block 35 must be specifically substantiated in comments. Comments must be verifiable.
Font must be 10 or 12 pitch (10 or 12 point) only. Use upper and lower case.

3 OF 59 FIRST CLASS PETTY OFFICERS. A proven performer in any situation, Petty Officer Allen is an outstanding Yeomen and leader. Select to Chief Petty Officer.
- ADMINISTRATIVE EXPERT. As Admin Department LPO, his supervision resulted in the admin office receiving an overall score of 97 percent during the Fleet Examination Group inspection (FEG). Processed over 500 pieces of correspondence while providing outstanding customer service between the Sailor and Admin.
- COMMAND LEADER. Hand-picked by the Executive Officer to act as the Mess Decks Master at Arms. As Mess Decks Master at Arms, he led 30 Food Service Attendants and enforced the highest standards among the crew. His actions were recognized by Supply Department and NEY inspectors that MOBILE BAY is an exemplary ship!
- TEAM PLAYER. As a Damage Control Training Team member he was essential in the command passing their Final Evaluation Problem with an overall score of 91 percent. 6 Sailors advanced to the next higher pay grade and retention of 95% of department.
- TOP PERFORMER. Only person in Admin Department to qualify as Combat System Officer of the Watch.
Petty Officer Allen is a self-starter whose leadership skills are needed in today's fast paced Navy. The deep respect he has achieved from each member of the department manifests his superlative qualities with integrity and professional knowledge. He should be promoted ahead of his peers and he has my Highest recommendation for selection to Chief Petty Officer. Select NOW!
*CMD Command Diversity Coordinator -12, FCPOA President-9. These two collateral duties were mentioned in block 29, but not in block 43. These two collateral duties will have no bearing at the Chief Petty Officer Selection Board, because they are not mentioned anywhere in block 43.

---

44. QUALIFICATIONS/ACHIEVEMENTS – Education, awards, community involvement, etc., during this period.

Awards: United States Military Apprenticeship Program, Letter of Appreciation. QUALS. Combat Systems Officer of the Watch, 9mm pistol, M500 shotgun. COURSES COMPL: Hazardous Substance Incident Response Management Course.

Promotion Recommendation	NOB	Significant Problems	Progressing	Promotable	Must Promote	Early Promote
45.						X
46. Summary	XXXXXX	0	0	21	27	11

YN1 (SW) Allen's last five PSR's

From 111609 To 111510

PG	Duty Station Name	Duty Type	From	To	# of Months	Reporting Senior Name	PG	Title
E6	CG 53 Mobile Bay	Leading Petty Officer	111609	111510	12	Cottam A J	06	CO

Associated Grades for the Above Duty Dates													
Members Trait Grade					Avereages for Trait				Promotion Recommendation				Misc
1	2	3	4	5	IND	SUM	R/S	CUM	SP	PR	P	MP	EP	RPT Type
0	0	0	4	3	4.42	4.12	137	3.78					X	RG
									0	0	14	18	10	

From 111608 To 111509

PG	Duty Station Name	Duty Type	From	To	# of Months	Reporting Senior Name	PG	Title
E6	CG 53 Mobile Bay	Leading Petty Officer	111608	111509	12	Deneale S V	06	CO

Associated Grades for the Above Duty Dates													
Members Trait Grade					Avereages for Trait				Promotion Recommendation				Misc
1	2	3	4	5	IND	SUM	R/S	CUM	SP	PR	P	MP	EP	RPT Type
0	0	0	4	3	4.29	4.17	272	4.04					X	RG
									0	0	12	16	9	

From 042108 To 111508

PG	Duty Station Name	Duty Type	From	To	# of Months	Reporting Senior Name	PG	Title
E6	CG 53 Mobile Bay	Workcenter Supervisor	042108	111508	07	Deneale S V	06	CO

Associated Grades for the Above Duty Dates

Members Trait Grade					Avereages for Trait				Promotion Recommendation					Misc
1	2	3	4	5	IND	SUM	R/S	CUM	SP	PR	P	MP	EP	RPT Type
0	0	3	2	2	3.86	4.14	168	4.03			X			RG
									0	0	11	17	8	

From 111607 To 042008

PG	Duty Station Name	Duty Type	From	To	# of Months	Reporting Senior Name	PG	Title
E6	PSD Yokosuka, Japan	Workcenter Supervisor	111607	042008	05	Gale, D J	06	CO

Associated Grades for the Above Duty Dates

Members Trait Grade					Avereages for Trait				Promotion Recommendation					Misc
1	2	3	4	5	IND	SUM	R/S	CUM	SP	PR	P	MP	EP	RPT Type
0	0	0	6	1	4.14	4.14	261	4.07				X		RG
									0	0	0	1	0	

From 111606 To 111507

PG	Duty Station Name	Duty Type	From	To	# of Months	Reporting Senior Name	PG	Title
E6	PSD Yokosuka, Japan	Workcenter Supervisor	111606	111507	12	Gale, D J	06	CO

Associated Grades for the Above Duty Dates

Members Trait Grade					Avereages for Trait				Promotion Recommendation					Misc
1	2	3	4	5	IND	SUM	R/S	CUM	SP	PR	P	MP	EP	RPT Type
0	0	2	3	2	4.00	4.29	181	4.07			X			RG
									0	0	7	11	6	

YN1 (SW/AW) Robbins' most recent evaluation

29. Primary/Collateral/Watchstanding duties (Enter primary duty abbreviations in box.)
ADMIN LPO — PRI: Military Administration/Command and Staff LPO-12. Supervised 18 personnel in support of pay and personnel for 12,000 officers and enlisted Sailors from the station and tenants. COLL: CMD Funeral and Honors Detail Coord-12, FCPOA President-9, Installation Training Team Member-12. Watch Bill Coord-8. WATCH: CDO-12.

43. COMMENTS ON PERFORMANCE. *All 1.0 marks, three 2.0 marks, and 2.0 marks in Block 35 must be specifically substantiated in comments. Comments must be verifiable.
Font must be 10 0r 12 pitch (10 or 12 point) only. Use upper and lower case.

*** 1 OF 62 FIRST CLASS PETTY OFFICERS. SELECT FOR CHIEF NOW! ***
YN1 (SW/AW) Robbins is a superb leader and manager who has significantly improved the operational effectiveness of his Department. Selected as the PSD Norfolk Sailor of the Year, FY 2010.
- PROFESSIONAL EXPERT. As Admin Department LPO, processed over 9,000 pieces of correspondence, while updating over 100 command instructions and expertly tracked a TADTAR budget of $20,000. As the watch Bill Coordinator, meticulously managed 75 duty section personnel. Key player is success of HURREX as ITT member.
COMMUNITY LEADER. As the FCPOA President, he was instrumental in raising over $3K in various fundraisers for the Navy Ball. He coordinated and led 36 Sailors who provided over 280 man-hours refurbishing a local public school, saving the community over $10,000 in commercial contracts and equipment.
- TEAM PLAYER. As the Funeral and Honors Coordinator, he was directly responsible for training and supervising 18 Sailors, while coordinating over 250 funeral honors and color guard ceremonies with pride and professionalism.
- IMPRESSIVE MENTOR. The outstanding care he shows for his Sailors in the department resulted in the selection of 1 JSOY, SOQ, and 1 BJOQ and 6 personnel selected for advancement.
Enrolled 6 Sailors in college and 2 earned Associates Degree.
Petty Officer Robbins is an extremely and dedicated and effective leader who is always ahead of the action while ensuring mission accomplishment. He should be promoted ahead of his contemporaries. HE HAS MY STRONGEST RECOMMENDATION FOR SELECTION TO CHIEF PETTY OFFICER. SELECT HIM NOW! 43. COMMENTS ON PERFORMANCE. *All

44. QUALIFICATIONS/ACHIEVEMENTS – Education, awards, community involvement, etc., during this period.
Education: Bachelor of Science from Ashford University. Completed Project Management, Calculus towards Master's Degree. Awarded: NCM, NAM (3rd), MOVSM, Letter of Appreciation 1st Baptist Church and Pleasant Grove Elementary School.

Promotion Recommendation	NOB	Significant Problems	Progressing	Promotable	Must Promote	Early Promote
45.						X
46. Summary	XXXXXX	0	0	21	24	17

YN1 (SW/AW) Robbins' last 5 PSRs

From 111609 To 111510

PG	Duty Station Name	Duty Type	From	To	# of Months	Reporting Senior Name	PG	Title
E6	PSD Norfolk, VA	Leading Petty Officer	111609	111510	12	Bradford, J. D.	06	CO

Associated Grades for the Above Duty Dates													
Members Trait Grade					Avereages for Trait				Promotion Recommendation				Misc
1	2	3	4	5	IND	SUM	R/S	CUM	SP	PR	P	MP	EP	RPT Type
0	0	0	2	5	4.71	4.02	347	3.99					X	RG
									0	0	21	24	17	

From 111608 To 111509

PG	Duty Station Name	Duty Type	From	To	# of Months	Reporting Senior Name	PG	Title
E6	PSD Norfolk, VA	Leading Petty Officer	111608	111509	12	Bradford, J. D.	06	CO

Associated Grades for the Above Duty Dates													
Members Trait Grade					Avereages for Trait				Promotion Recommendation				Misc
1	2	3	4	5	IND	SUM	R/S	CUM	SP	PR	P	MP	EP	RPT Type
0	0	0	5	2	4.29	4.01	291	3.96				X		RG
									0	0	17	21	16	

From 031608 To 111508

PG	Duty Station Name	Duty Type	From	To	# of Months	Reporting Senior Name	PG	Title
E6	PSD Norfolk, VA	Educational Service Officer	031608	111508	08	Williams, J. W.	06	CO

Associated Grades for the Above Duty Dates															Misc
Members Trait Grade					Avereages for Trait				Promotion Recommendation						
1	2	3	4	5	IND	SUM	R/S	CUM	SP	PR	P	MP	EP	RPT Type	
0	0	1	4	2	4.14	4.12	217	4.02			X			RG	
									0	0	11	21	14		

From 021507 To 031508

PG	Duty Station Name	Duty Type	From	To	# of Months	Reporting Senior Name	PG	Title
E6	NEGB GTMO CUBA	Platoon Leader	021407	031508	13	Adams, K. S.	05	XO

Associated Grades for the Above Duty Dates															Misc
Members Trait Grade					Avereages for Trait				Promotion Recommendation						
1	2	3	4	5	IND	SUM	R/S	CUM	SP	PR	P	MP	EP	RPT Type	
0	0	0	2	5	4.71	4.29	261	4.09					X	RG	
									0	0	44	58	32		

From 031606 To 021407

PG	Duty Station Name	Duty Type	From	To	# of Months	Reporting Senior Name	PG	Title
E6	CG 51 T S GATES	Leading Petty Officer	031606	021407	11	Eyer, K. S.	05	XO

Associated Grades for the Above Duty Dates															Misc
Members Trait Grade					Avereages for Trait				Promotion Recommendation						
1	2	3	4	5	IND	SUM	R/S	CUM	SP	PR	P	MP	EP	RPT Type	
0	0	0	3	4	4.57	4.57	191	4.07					X	RG	
									0	0	0	0	1		

YN1 (SW) Allen's Mid-term counseling

43. COMMENTS ON PERFORMANCE. *All 1.0, three 2.0 marks, and 2.0 marks in Block 35 must be specifically substantiated in comments. Comments must be verifiable. Font must be 10 or 12 Pitch (10 or 12 point) only. Use upper and lower case.

Strengths:
1.   Organized and resourceful. (General) Organized and resourceful of what? Needs to be more specific.
2.   Maintains standards. (General) Maintain standards are not a strength. This should be an area for improvement that states what standards are expected and how to improve.
3.   Completes tasks well before deadline. (Specific)

Areas for Improvement:
1.   Enroll in college. (General) Enroll in college is a good area for improvement, but should be more specific such as a start date.
2.   Take over as the Command Mentorship Coordinator. (Specific).
3.   Make more use of idle time at work. (General) Too vague, needs to be more specific and how to improve.
4.   Improve communication skills. (General) This statement is too general. Does the Sailor need to improve communication up and down the chain of command, or within the department, when assigning duties, etc)?

Now that we've seen Petty Officer Allen's Mid-term counseling were you able to see why it was generalized. Could it have been more specific? How would you have made any changes? Are your Mid-term evaluations like Petty Officer Allen's? If so, what changes would you make and how? We will now look at Petty Officer Robbins' Mid-term evaluation below.

YN1 (SW/AW) Robbins' Mid-term counseling

43. COMMENTS ON PERFORMANCE. *All 1.0, three 2.0 marks, and 2.0 marks in Block 35 must be specifically substantiated in comments. Comments must be verifiable. Font must be 10 or 12 Pitch (10 or 12 point) only. Use upper and lower case.

Strengths:
1.   Received outstanding medium on most recent PFA (Specific).
2.   Provides first rate advancement training for all Sailors. Sailors enjoy competition and camaraderie at all advancement jeopardy and stump the Chief events (Specific).
3.   As the FCPOA President, remains very proactive in command and community events setting the example for all others to emulate (Specific).

Areas for Improvement:
1.   Improve your communication skills with junior Sailors. All information from the chain of command doesn't always reach them. Besides communicating go back and verify they received and understand (Specific).
Don't over task yourself with education, collateral duties, and other duties which may hinder your ability to lead your Sailors (Specific).

Sample Evaluation for MA1 (SW) Joe Navy

Following is an example of an evaluation which may sound good, but doesn't have any real substance. After reading it, see how you could make it better, or do you think this is a good evaluation?

29. Primary/Collateral/Watchstanding duties (Enter primary duty abbreviations in box.)

DIVISION LPO

PRI: XX Divisional Leading Petty Officer-12. Supervised 38 personnel in support of Antiterrorism/Force Protection and Physical Security for over 3,000 officers and enlisted Sailors from the station and tenants. COLL: CMD Investigator-12, FCPOA Treasurer-12, Installation Training Team Member-12. WATCH: Command Duty Officer-8.

43. COMMENTS ON PERFORMANCE. *All 1.0 marks, three 2.0 marks, and 2.0 marks in Block 35 must be specifically substantiated in comments. Comments must be verifiable.
Font must be 10 0r 12 pitch (10 or 12 point) only. Use upper and lower case.

MA1 (SW) Navy is a superb leader and manager who significantly improved the operational effectiveness of his Division and the command. He's always sought out for his technical expertise and military knowledge..
As an exceptional leader, manager and organizer, Petty Officer Navy fosters high morale and a total winning attitude and spirit motivating others to achieve or exceed unit goals. He sets high standards for conduct and performance.
His meticulous attention to detail and outstanding attributes make the Sailor for all others to emulate. His sound advice and supervisory skills have made him a vital asset within the command.
His expert knowledge in Anti-terrorism/Force Protection and Physical Security Measures are second to none, ensuring the command and all tenant commands comply with command and naval instructions.
As the Leading Petty Officer, he Provides positive direction, sound advice, firm guidance, and wise counsel to all Sailors within his division. Always produces positive results.
Motivate his sailors instead of driving them to perform to the best of their ability, both as individuals and as a division. His knowledge, experience and military bearing make him a role model LPO.
Petty Officer Navy possesses all the attributes needed in todays faced pace Navy. His outstanding leadership skills coupled with his extensive military knowledge instill the Navy core values of

Promotion Recommendation	NOB	Significant Problems	Progressing	Promotable	Must Promote	Early Promote
45.						X
46. Summary	XXXXXX	0	0	21	24	17

The Importance of Well-Written Evaluations

Part of being well-rounded with regard to evaluations is knowing how to write them yourself. As a leader, being well-versed in writing evaluations on others sets you up for success as well. Conversely, an inability to write great evaluations on others could also be the difference between being selected or not selected at your own chief petty officer selection board.

Even if you become a chief petty officer but are still weak at writing evaluations, your job will be much harder when it comes to submitting evaluations for the sailors within your division, department, or command. If you're weak at writing evaluations, if you're unable to write evaluations that effectively portray a sailor as a "must promote" or "early promote," it will have a negative effect on your sailors when they're evaluated at their ranking boards. If you don't know how to write the worthy attributes and significant achievements of a first class petty officer into his or her evaluation, the chief petty officer selection board may simply take your badly written evaluation and set it aside. This can have a negative effect on you when your next selection board reviews the evaluations you wrote.

It's difficult enough for a first class petty officer to take the exam and become chief petty officer board-eligible. Having badly written evaluations in front of the chief petty officer selection board will not do anyone justice. And a particular board could be that petty officer's best, or even his only, chance to be selected. How would you feel if he failed to be selected because your evaluations didn't capture his attributes, or were so badly written they were never read?

If the chief petty officer selection board is considering you for selection, reading your badly written evaluations on others may show that you're not ready for advancement yet. Although the evaluations you write won't be the only factor the board uses to select the best candidates, don't let this be the factor that makes the difference in whether you're selected. You want your record to speak for itself—so make sure it's well-written.

Being able to write good evaluations is an essential part of being a chief petty officer. As a first class petty officer, you should already be well-versed in writing evaluations. If you're not, seek training from your chiefs.

Chapter 4

Previous Trends

Exams and Eligibility

We're going to take a look at the chief petty officer advancement exams for fiscal years 2010, 2011, and 2012 and their quotas. The first results are for active duty chief petty officers only (the results for Full-Time Support and Reserve component sailors will be covered later in this chapter). The tables and graphs show trends for each rating, with the results for each year. I've also added a few pictures of first class petty officers who were selected from their respective commands over the last several years. The results of the chief petty officer selection boards get sent out via message, or you can see the results on the Navy Personnel Command website. The website also offers the precepts listing the areas each chief petty officer selection board looked at.

First class petty officers are selected based on their records examined by the chief petty officer selection board. An important factor to remember is that if you fail to become board-eligible, everything that might have made you competitive that year is locked away from the selection board, and you may have lost your only chance to be selected. Although you may be competitive among your peers, the chief petty officer selection board will never know—the board can only select from among those sailors who are board-eligible.

Each year the chief petty officer selection board assembles to rate each sailor among his or her peers within their perspective ratings. Knowing how the board grades sailors will give you the best opportunity to be selected. This process can only begin for you if you score high enough on the E7 advancement exam. Good evaluations also make up a large portion of your overall score. These two areas can decide your fate as far as being board-eligible.

You can find the information you need to study for your advancement exam in the bibliography for your rating; this resource can also provide insight about which areas to focus on in general. I always recommended that my sailors take plenty of time when studying for the advancement exam, starting at least four months prior to the test day. I also recommended studying the areas they *didn't* know; some sailors use up all their time re-studying material they already know. You need to study well enough for the E7 advancement exam to become board-eligible.

Examples

When I was the leading chief petty officer at the Security Department at Naval Air Station Brunswick, Maine, I had a first class petty officer who had decided to get out of the Navy. He informed me he wasn't going to take the E7 exam because it would be a waste of time and effort. I sat him down and explained that, first, if he didn't take the test I would write him up for unauthorized absence. Second, I also counseled him to never burn his bridges, and to never fail to take advantage of opportunities. After all, things happen in life, and anything can happen between now and the time your terminal leave ends.

This first class petty officer took the advancement exam—and scored in the 97th percentile. He became board-eligible. Then, while he was on terminal leave, he found out the job he wanted would not pay his bills because too much would come out of his

Newly selected chief petty officers from Naval Station Norfolk, Virginia. These are just four of the sailors selected from the 2008 fiscal year cycle. Being selected as a chief petty officer is a great achievement, but with it comes even greater responsibility. Being a chief petty officer will be one of the hardest jobs you'll ever have, providing many challenges. It will also be one of the most rewarding—ask any chief petty officer. *James C. Glass*

When I was pinned to chief petty officer in 2004, I was on an Individual Augmentee tour in Iraq. Becoming a chief petty officer was my proudest moment during my entire Navy career, even more rewarding than being selected to senior chief or even master chief (although both of the latter were also very rewarding). Being a chief petty officer was the hardest job I ever had but also the most rewarding. There's no greater satisfaction than leading, mentoring, training, and helping sailors. The satisfaction I received from seeing sailors succeed was priceless. The day this picture was taken I had lost 25 pounds since arriving in Baghdad, Iraq, almost six months earlier. *James C. Glass*

These are the other chiefs who were pinned with me in Iraq. They were also on Individual Augmentee tours. We built a bond with each other while going through the transition from first class petty officer to chief petty officer. Although we have gone our different ways in our careers since then, I still stay in contact with them. (You'll notice in both pictures that we're not wearing our covers. This is because we were in a no-cover area, of which there were many in Iraq. We were pinned in our khaki uniforms, but our uniform of the day was the desert camouflage uniform.) Standing, from left: Chief Petty Officers Glass, Steven, Williams, and Matthews. There's no better feeling than the day your anchors are pinned on your uniform. This was the happiest moment in each of our Navy careers. If you ask any other chief in the Navy, I guarantee he or she will tell you the same thing. *James C. Glass*

The 36 first class petty officers who took the FY12 chief petty officer advancement exam at Naval Support Activity, Lakehurst, New Jersey. *Herbert Kelton*

paycheck each month for medical benefits. So instead he decided to reenlist in the Navy. And when the chief petty officer results came out, his name was on the list. With the high level of competition at the chief petty officer selection board each year, this may have been his only opportunity to be selected. He thanked me for helping him see the bigger picture.

The same is true regarding Petty Officer Allen and Petty Officer Robbins. Petty Officer Allen has studied for his exam and been board-eligible each time he's taken it, but relies on wishful thinking instead of pursuing goals aimed at making him more competitive at the selection board. On the other hand, while Petty Officer Robbins has become board-eligible, he's also made it an overall goal to be selected, and has taken the time to focus on and pursue the intermediate goals that will make him more competitive among his peers.

Knowing the goals that will help you succeed is very important. Sometimes our existing goals are not in line with what our goals need to be. You may *feel* you know what's best, but you may not have the experience, knowledge, or insight to know what you should *actually* focus on. This is where your mentor or a career development board can play a vital role in the success or failure of your naval career.

When I was a chief petty officer, I had a first class petty officer who was the mentorship coordinator for the department. He gathered all the useful tools that would benefit mentors as well as protégés. The only thing he lacked was judgment as to who should be a mentor. When he came to me with his proposed list, he had first class petty officers listed as mentors for other first class petty officers—and I informed him this couldn't happen. When he asked why, I replied, how can a first class petty officer help another first class petty officer get selected to chief petty officer? All I had to do was ask this simple question and he understood what I meant without going into further detail. It would have been like the blind leading the blind.

TABLE 2: Fiscal Year 2012 Active Duty CPO Quotas

This table represents the fiscal year 2012 chief selection board results for active-duty sailors. Of the more than 19,500 first class petty officers who were CPO board eligible, 3,571 were selected during this cycle, approximately 18.74 percent.

RATING	FY 2012 QUOTA	RATING	FY 2012 QUOTA	RATING	FY 2012 QUOTA
ABE	23	CTM	18	MA	74
ABF	25	CTN	19	MC	21
ABH	37	CTR	78	MM	83
AC	34	CTT	22	MME	31
AD	106	DC	42	MMN GRP 1	82
AE	66	EA	0	MMN GRP 2	73
AG	28	EM	76	MMW	20
AM	132	EMN GRP 1	44	MN	26
AME	33	EMN GRP 2	23	MR	10
AO	102	EN	100	MT	15
AS	6	EO	2	MU GRP 1	12
ATI	38	EOD	60	MU GRP 2	10
ATO	55	ET	78	NCC	16
AWF	13	ETN GRP 1	54	NCR	31
AWO	26	ETN GRP 2	16	ND	31
AWR	14	ETR	26	OS	75
AWS	17	ETV	41	PR	23
AWV	9	FC	36	PS	85
AZ	46	FC Aegis	53	QM	27
BM	61	FT	35	RP	7
BU	3	GM	72	SB	31
CE	2	GSE	35	SH	17
CM	2	GSM	36	SO	78
CS GRP 1	36	HM	190	STG	50
CSGRP 2	63	HT	53	STS	39
CTI GRP 1	6	IC	26	SW	1
CTI GRP 2	4	IS	25	UT	3
CTI GRP 3	3	IT	118	YN GRP 1	19
CTI GRP 4	1	LN	7	YN GRP 2	68
CTI GRP 5	3	LS GRP 1	31		
CTI GRP 6	2	LS GRP 2	99	**TOTAL**	3571

TABLE 3: Fiscal Year 2011 Active Duty CPO Quotas

The table above represents the fiscal year 2011 chief petty officer selection board results for active-duty sailors. Overall, of the more than 19,500 first class sailors who were CPO board eligible, 3,673 first class petty officers were selected, 18.84 percent.

RATING	FY 2011 QUOTA	RATING	FY 2011 QUOTA	RATING	FY 2011 QUOTA
ABE	5	CTM	12	MA	76
ABF	4	CTN	31	MC	16
ABH	13	CTR	75	MM	52
AC	25	CTT	39	MME	35
AD	87	DC	29	MMN GRP 1	65
AE	63	EA	7	MMN GRP 2	50
AG	21	EM	12	MMW	23
AM	90	EMN GRP 1	49	MN	20
AME	19	EMN GRP 2	20	MR	5
AO	87	EN	89	MT	49
AS	24	EO	24	MU GRP 1	7
ATI	38	EOD	53	MU GRP 2	6
ATO	55	ET	74	NCC	38
AWF	13	ETN GRP 1	41	NCR	37
AWO	19	ETN GRP 2	18	ND	30
AWR	20	ETR	45	OS	118
AWS	8	ETV	50	PR	20
AWV	10	FC	75	PS	52
AZ	44	FC Aegis	35	QM	72
BM	76	FT	40	RP	12
BU	22	GM	40	SB	32
CE	11	GSE	20	SH	16
CM	26	GSM	22	SO	88
CS GRP 1	20	HM	220	STG	39
CSGRP 2	73	HT	43	STS	63
CTI GRP 1	5	IC	18	SW	13
CTI GRP 2	10	IS	55	UT	18
CTI GRP 3	2	IT	200	YN GRP 1	9
CTI GRP 4	3	LN	18	YN GRP 2	107
CTI GRP 5	3	LS GRP 1	15		
CTI GRP 6	0	LS GRP 2	140	**TOTAL**	**3673**

TABLE 4: Fiscal Year 2010 Active Duty CPO Quotas

These fiscal year 2010 chief petty officer results for active-duty sailors show how many first class petty officers took the exam and how many were chief petty officer board eligible. This provides a fuller picture than the fiscal year 2011 and 2012 results given previously. A total of 19,701 first class petty officers were chief petty officer board eligible. Of these, 3697 were selected, an overall result of 18.77 percent during this cycle. If you have any questions about how the chief petty officer board made its selections, go to the Navy Personnel Command (NPC) website or contact your Education Service Officer. Either can provide information that shows how the process works. The NPC will show you the precepts for that year's chief petty officer board selection process. Although the Wheel of Success has more specific information, the precepts provide a great foundation.

RATING	FY 2010 CPO BOARD ELIGIBLE	FY 2010 CPO SELECT-ED QUOTA	CPO %	RATING	FY 2010 CPO BOARD ELIGIBLE	FY 2010 CPO SELECT-ED QUOTA	CPO %
ABE	129	33	25.58%	BU	164	25	15.24%
ABF	82	16	19.51%	CE	116	16	13.79%
ABH	198	46	23.23%	CM	162	13	8.02%
AC	232	25	10.78%	CS GRP 1	63	20	31.75%
AD	436	100	22.99%	CSGRP 2	395	75	18.99%
AE	284	66	23.24%	CTI GRP 1	31	8	25.81%
AG	130	15	11.54%	CTI GRP 2	21	0	0.00%
AM	580	71	12.24%	CTI GRP 3	37	6	16.22%
AME	128	21	16.41%	CTI GRP 4	19	2	10.53%
AO	466	83	17.81%	CTI GRP 5	36	3	8.33%
AS	134	15	11.19%	CTI GRP 6	23	8	34.78%
ATI	251	72	28.78%	CTM	73	1	1.37%
ATO	348	100	28.67%	CTN	95	31	32.63%
AWF	133	22	16.54%	CTR	326	78	23.93%
AWO	110	22	20.00%	CTT	249	57	22.89%
AWR	86	7	8.14%	DC	220	21	9.55%
AWS	93	6	6.45%	EA	22	8	36.36%
AWV	74	26	35.14%	EM	254	53	20.87%
AZ	169	33	19.53%	EMN GRP 1	206	37	17.96%
BM	315	89	28.25%	EMN GRP 2	88	15	17.05%

TABLE 4, continued

RATING	FY 2010 CPO BOARD ELIGIBLE	FY 2010 CPO SELECT-ED QUOTA	CPO %	RATING	FY 2010 CPO BOARD ELIGIBLE	FY 2010 CPO SELECT-ED QUOTA	CPO %
EN	436	22	5.05%	MMW	67	46	68.66%
EO	135	25	18.52%	MN	55	26	47.27%
EOD	115	62	53.91%	MR	71	0	0.00%
ET	515	55	10.68%	MT	59	22	24.72%
ETN GRP 1	122	44	36.07%	MU GRP 1	62	6	9.68%
ETN GRP 2	93	11	11.83%	MU GRP 2	36	8	22.22%
ETR	129	33	25.58%	NCC	176	29	16.48%
ETV	122	66	64.10%	NCR	128	79	61.72%
FC	330	56	16.97%	ND	106	44	41.51%
FC Aegis	206	17	8.25%	OS	523	91	17.40%
FT	97	33	34.02%	PC	50	8	16.00%
GM	392	35	8.93%	PR	145	9	6.21%
GSE	93	15	16.13%	PS	416	24	5.77%
GSM	166	39	23.49%	QM	182	21	11.54%
HM	1248	296	23.72%	RP	84	14	16.67%
HT	235	8	3.40%	SB	69	31	44.93%
IC	197	8	4.57%	SH	165	26	15.15%
IS	206	91	39.32%	SK GRP 1	34	6	17.65%
IT	1095	170	15.53%	SK GRP 2	610	177	29.02%
LN	93	14	15.22%	SO	311	90	28.94%
MA	734	65	8.86%	STS	221	37	16.74%
MC	133	17	12.78%	SW	78	11	14.10%
MM	389	114	29.31%	UT	110	4	3.64%
MMN GRP 1	384	51	13.28%	YN GRP 1	48	13	27.08%
MMN GRP 2	272	37	13.60%	YN GRP 2	544	108	19.85%
MME	164	34	20.73%	**TOTAL**	**19701**	**3697**	**18.77**

TABLE 5: Fiscal Year 2012 Full-Time Support CPO Quotas

This table represents the fiscal year (FY) 2012 chief petty officer selection board results for full-time support quotas. In FY12, 174 first class petty officers were selected; in the previous year, 192 were selected. This decrease of 18 in sailors selected to chief represents over a nine percent decline from the previous year.

RATING	QUOTA	RATING	QUOTA
ADC	10	ENC	4
AEC	3	ETC	3
AMC	11	HMC	19
AMEC	1	HTC	0
AOC	6	ICC	0
ASC	5	ITC	7
ATIC	1	LSC	11
ATOC	5	MRC	0
AWFC	0	NCC	6
AZC	2	NCR	18
BMC	6	PRC	3
CSC	1	PSC	23
DCC	2	YNC	25
EMC	2	**FY12 TOTAL**	174

TABLE 6: Fiscal Year 2011 Full-Time Support CPO Quotas

This table represents the fiscal year (FY) 2011 chief selection board results for full-time support quotas. In FY11, 192 first class petty officers were selected; in FY10, 233 were selected. The decrease of 41 in sailors selected to chief represents over a 17 percent decline from the previous year.

RATING	QUOTA	RATING	QUOTA
ADC	6	ENC	10
AEC	8	ETC	2
AMC	14	HMC	15
AMEC	4	HTC	0
AOC	6	ICC	0
ASC	3	ITC	4
ATIC	4	LSC	12
ATOC	9	MRC	0
AWFC	5	NCC	3
AZC	10	NCR	16
BMC	6	PRC	0
CSC	2	PSC	20
DCC	6	YNC	22
EMC	5	**FY11 TOTAL**	**192**

TABLE 7: Fiscal Year 2010 Full-Time Support CPO Quotas

This table represents the fiscal year (FY) 2010 chief selection board results for full-time support quotas. In that year, the chief petty officer selection board selected 233; but over FY10-12, the average was 199 per year.

RATING	QUOTA	RATING	QUOTA
ADC	11	ENC	15
AEC	7	ETC	4
AMC	15	HMC	20
AMEC	4	HTC	0
AOC	6	ICC	0
ASC	3	ITC	7
ATIC	4	LSC	0
ATOC	12	MRC	2
AWFC	0	NCC	2
AZC	6	NCR	30
BMC	10	PRC	3
CSC	2	PSC	22
DCC	8	SKC	15
EMC	10	YNC	17
		FY10 TOTAL	**233**

TABLE 8: Fiscal Year 2012 Selective Reserve CPO Quotas

This table represents the fiscal year (FY) 2012 chief petty officer selection board results for Selective Reserve sailors. There were 721 chief petty officer quotas available, 19 fewer than the sailors selected in FY10, a decline of over two percent.

RATING	FY 2012 QUOTA	RATING	FY 2012 QUOTA	RATING	FY 2012 QUOTA
ABEC	1	CTMC	0	MAC	57
ABFC	0	CTNC	0	MCC	8
ABHC	5	CTRC	9	MMC	6
ACC	0	CTTC	8	MMEC	1
ADC	12	DCC	0	MMWC	1
AEC	10	EAC	0	MNC	1
AGC	10	EMC	10	MRC	10
AMC	5	ENC	9	NDC	4
AMEC	3	EOC	25	OSC	28
AOC	0	EODC	3	PRC	1
ASC	0	ETC	0	PSC	7
ATIC	5	ETRC	0	QMC	11
ATOC	6	ETVC	0	RPC	6
AWFC	3	FCC	1	SBC	10
AWOC	6	GMC	15	SHC	1
AWRC	0	GSEC	1	SOC	9
AWSC	2	GSMC	0	STGC	0
AZC	4	HMC	80	STSC	3
BMC	59	HTC	8	SWC	9
BUC	16	ICC	0	UTC	4
CEC	12	ISC	44	YNC	51
CMC	15	ITC	37		
CSC	11	LNC	9		
CTIC	1	LSC	48	FY12 TOTAL	721

TABLE 9: Fiscal Year 2011 Selective Reserve CPO Quotas

This table represents the fiscal year (FY) 2011 chief petty officer selection board results for Selective Reserve sailors. There were 740 chief petty officer quotas available, 72 fewer than in the FY10, a decrease of over eight percent.

RATING	FY 2011 QUOTA	RATING	FY 2011 QUOTA	RATING	FY 2011 QUOTA
ABEC	2	CTMC	0	MAC	35
ABFC	3	CTNC	1	MCC	4
ABHC	3	CTRC	6	MMC	20
ACC	2	CTTC	7	MMEC	1
ADC	1	DCC	1	MMWC	1
AEC	9	EAC	5	MNC	5
AGC	12	EMC	16	MRC	15
AMC	5	ENC	8	NDC	2
AMEC	0	EOC	16	OSC	22
AOC	2	EODC	5	PRC	0
ASC	0	ETC	15	PSC	11
ATIC	1	ETRC	1	QMC	9
ATOC	1	ETVC	1	RPC	1
AWFC	6	FCC	4	SBC	8
AWOC	2	GMC	8	SHC	1
AWRC	1	GSEC	3	SOC	8
AWSC	1	GSMC	2	STGC	7
AZC	1	HMC	93	STSC	1
BMC	55	HTC	25	SWC	7
BUC	22	ICC	0	UTC	5
CEC	8	ISC	48	YNC	22
CMC	17	ITC	42	**FY11 TOTAL**	**740**
CSC	12	LNC	4		
CTIC	0	LSC	82		

TABLE 10: Fiscal Year 2010 Selective Reserve CPO Quotas

This table represents the fiscal year 2010 chief petty officer selection board results for Selective Reserve sailors. There were 812 chief petty officer quotas available.

RATING	FY 2010 QUOTA	RATING	FY 2010 QUOTA	RATING	FY 2010 QUOTA
ABEC	1	CTIC	0	MAC	55
ABFC	2	CTMC	0	MCC	14
ABHC	4	CTNC	6	MMC	24
ACC	1	CTRC	13	MMEC	1
ADC	5	CTTC	4	MMWC	1
AEC	12	DCC	0	MNC	3
AGC	10	EAC	0	MRC	9
AMC	7	EMC	17	NDC	2
AMEC	0	ENC	5	OSC	22
AOC	1	EOC	34	PCC	3
ASC	2	EODC	5	PRC	0
ATIC	1	ETC	26	PSC	12
ATOC	1	ETRC	1	QMC	7
AWFC	1	ETVC	1	RPC	1
AWOC	2	FCC	2	SBC	4
AWRC	0	GMC	6	SHC	0
AWSC	0	GSEC	1	SKC	61
AZC	1	GSMC	2	SOC	13
BMC	61	HMC	100	STGC	0
BUC	36	HTC	20	STSC	2
CEC	9	ICC	2	SWC	10
CMC	23	ISC	48	UTC	12
CSC	11	ITC	55	YNC	13
		LNC	4	**FY10 TOTAL**	**812**

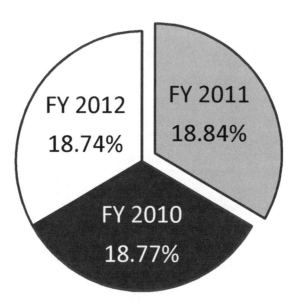

This chart shows the percentage of first class petty officers selected to chief petty officer over the past three advancement cycles. Although some ratings have seen significant changes, increasing or decreasing, the percentage of first class petty officers advanced to chief petty officer has remained fairly constant overall.

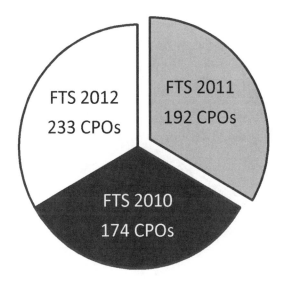

The chart above shows the overall number of full-time support first class petty officers selected to chief petty officer over the past three advancement cycles. Although some ratings have seen some significant changes, either increasing or decreasing, the overall percentage of first class petty officers being advanced to chief petty officer has declined dramatically. That is why it's important to be competitive among your peers.

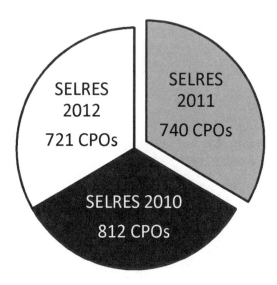

The chart shows the percentage of Selective Reserve first class petty officers selected to chief petty officer over the past three advancement cycles. Although some ratings have seen significant changes, either increasing or decreasing, the percentage of first class petty officers being advanced to chief petty officer has remained relatively constant overall.

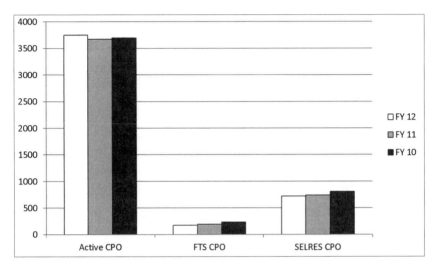

The bar graph chart illustrates all of the chief petty officers selected during the entire selection cycles for FY10-12. It displays the overall results as well as the trend over the three years. The graph combines the results for the active-duty, full-time support, and Selective Reserve components previously illustrated in separate pie charts.

Chapter 5

The Wheel of Success

A Review of Goals

The "Wheel of Success" is a tool you can use to track your career. It will help you align your goals with what you need to do to become more competitive among your peers; it will help make you a well-rounded sailor. You must break out in other areas besides being the best technician, logistician, or administrator.

To briefly review Chapter 1 on goals: the overall goal of becoming a chief petty officer is a good one. But a goal is just that; to be successful, you must also achieve your goals. In goal-setting, you must know what your goals are, they must be realistic, and you must have a plan in place to achieve them. Successfully setting and achieving some goals will give you confidence, paving the way to more achievement. You should have at least short-and long-term goals, but mid-term goals are okay too. One way to check whether your goals are properly aligned with your career is by having periodic career development boards. They'll help you see where you currently stand on achieving your goals and what you need to

Career Development Board NSA Lakehurst, New Jersey
Herbert Kelton

focus on to achieve them. This includes not only professional goals but personal ones as well.

When I was command master chief at Naval Weapons Station Earle, I decided to go back to college and earn my bachelor's degree. I thought the degree would help me after I retired from the Navy. I had been a master-at-arms to that point in my career, and thought I would get my degree in criminal justice. However, in conversation with an academic counselor at my intended college, he asked me whether I would be a master-at-arms for the remainder of my career. I replied that I was going to be a command master chief, a role more focused on leadership and administration. As a result of that conversation, I changed my plan and got my degree in applied management. The point is that when I began the process I was sure that getting my degree in criminal justice was the way to go, but by talking with the academic counselor I realized I should go in a different direction. I'm certain I ended up making the right decision.

You may be asking yourself the same question. You may be undecided on what you want to do or how you want to pursue it. Having people you can trust to whom you can turn will help you get on the road to success. And if you find yourself in a position to do the same for someone else, you should. After all, it's not always about you, it's about the bigger picture. This is why the chiefs' mess has been successful for so many years. Chiefs understand that it's not about us, it's about our sailors and how we can help them become successful. If you think it's all about you, you should either change your ways or expect a long, bumpy road ahead.

The Wheel

The Wheel of Success consists of ten distinct areas to focus on to become more competitive among your peers. Study the ten areas, focus on your goals, and set about achieving them.
The ten areas:

1. Awards

2. Collateral Duties

3. Command Involvement

4. Community Involvement

5. Diversity

6. Education

7. Sailorization

8. Warfare Qualifications

9. Sustained Superior Performance

10. Proven Deckplate Leadership

Over the course of this book we'll cover each of these sections in greater detail. At the end of the book is Appendix I, which contains a Wheel of Success diagram and breaks each section down into subcategories.

Career Development Board NSA Lakehurst, New Jersey

Herbert Kelton

A points scheme applies to the Wheel. Each section is worth a maximum of ten points. A sailor has the opportunity to earn a maximum of 100 points by completing all the sections. Breaking each section down shows you in detail how you can earn up to ten points within that section. If you focus too much on any one area, say, community service, and you achieve the maximum ten points but actually have enough community service to earn twenty-five points, you're giving up points in another area, say, education. The extra time and effort you're spending on community service might be the amount of time and effort needed to earn credits toward a college degree.

The purpose of the Wheel of Success is to tailor your efforts to the different areas. Your goals regarding them should be in line with your overall objective of becoming a chief petty officer. Aligning your goals to the Wheel of Success will make you more competitive among your peers. A career development board can also ensure that you're aligning your goals as needed within your rating or your respective community, thus setting you up for success.

The key to success is proper planning and consistency. It's easy to become too involved in one area, but the Wheel can help apportion your efforts between areas and keep you on track toward your goals. Being able to clearly see where you want to go, what the path is to get there, and what you need to do to go down that path is the way to achieve success, not depending on wishful thinking or pursuing goals that may not align with the precepts of the chief petty officer selection board.

The board precepts are usually the same each year, and in any case are generalized. In contrast, the Wheel of Success gives you specifics on what you need to achieve. The precepts provide a foundation and have been a useful tool over the years, but I believe the Wheel of Success is the next step for sailors who want to become more successful. The specifics within the Wheel help a sailor tailor his efforts in each area so as to provide focus on his career and alignment of his goals. Tailoring your own career plan will help you achieve your goal of becoming a chief petty officer. Use the Wheel!

Chapter 6

Awards

Levels of Recognition

Everyone likes recognition for their contributions—it's human nature. It feels good when we get recognition for doing a good job. For sailors, that good "job" can include contributions to the community as well as the command. Conversely, if you went above and beyond the call of duty to support your command and were not recognized for it, would you do it again?

Recognition for our accomplishments can come in many forms. Suppose you're an Electronics Technician who was able to troubleshoot and repair the Identify Friend or Foe antennae while the ship was in homeport. You found out what the problem was during the course of the workday, ordered the necessary parts, and got the antennae operational by the end of the workday. The parts were onboard, so you didn't need to casrep the parts (i.e., send a report). Should you be recognized for this action? If so, what recognition would be appropriate? A letter of commendation from the commanding officer? Maybe a Navy Achievement Medal

(NAM)? Or, if your department head gave you praise at quarters the next day, would that be recognition enough?

The answer varies depending on the particular command, how it conducts its awards boards, and how much time and energy your chain of command puts into supporting its people's actions. I was at a command where the executive officer, command master chief, department heads, and leading chief petty officers held awards boards every quarter; I was also at commands where the command master chief and the leading chief petty officers were the only ones at awards boards, which were held irregularly—one might be coming up in a month, or maybe next quarter, because there was no set schedule.

Let's say your department head chose to recognize you with praise at quarters the following morning in front of the entire department, or the commanding officer praised your actions over the 1MC announcing system. Would this give you satisfaction for your work? If so, would you continue to work hard? Or would you feel you deserved instead a letter of commendation or NAM from the commanding officer, or a flag letter of command from your immediate superior in command?

Because you performed the work, should you be the one to determine the standard of reward? No, you don't get to decide what kind of recognition you receive. The standard should already be set in place at each command, embodied in an instruction. That doesn't mean you'll necessarily receive the recognition you deserve. I've been at commands where, in my opinion, a first class petty officer deserved a Navy Commendation Medal (NCM) but didn't receive it because the command's award instruction stated that only department heads, the command master chief, and leading chief petty officers could receive NCMs. I went so far as to speak to the commanding officer about it, but he would not deviate from his instruction. I felt there should be exceptions to the rule; he did not.

If this happened to you, would it affect your motivation to continue to work hard; would the lack of what you considered proper recognition hold you back from fulfilling your full potential? Do you feel others are being recognized for their actions and you're not? I'm not saying this doesn't happen, because it does. However, what I saw in my career is that most sailors got the recognition they earned.

Here's a variant on the earlier scenario. Say you repaired the Identify Friend or Foe antennae while the ship was underway in the Persian Gulf. You worked more than 20 hours troubleshooting. The parts weren't available on board, so the command had to get them from another ship nearby. Would the same recognition that you would have received in the earlier scenario be enough of a reward now? Remember, the command has many options by which it can praise someone for a job well done: positive counseling; a letter of appreciation or commendation from the commanding officer; a flag letter of commendation; the NAM; the NCM; or even higher.

Sometimes, despite all these options, sailors get no recognition at all. Perhaps their chain of command just doesn't take the time, or those in the chain have poor writing skills, or the chain loses track of the paperwork. Sometimes the chain of command wants you to write your own award, but I've never asked a sailor to do that. Some may feel this is a form of training for the sailor on how to write awards, but I feel a sailor shouldn't have to write his or her own award. To me, this is pure laziness on the part of the chain of command, an example of bad leadership.

Do you feel that in order for someone else to be recognized, you must also be recognized? Proper recognition should be more about your sailors than yourself. "Service before self" is a phrase that reminds each of us that it's not about us, it's about the Navy. "Take care of your sailors, and they'll take care of you." This is the approach your chiefs and your chain of command expect of you. The chiefs' mess has always reinforced the idea that "I didn't get here on my own." Although I reached the rank of master chief petty officer, I didn't get there on my own; and any chief, senior chief, or master chief will tell you the same. Develop your own leadership and that of others by taking care of your sailors.

Types of Recognition

Positive Counseling Sheet

You may have received positive counseling during your career, but have you ever received a positive counseling sheet from your superiors? Have you ever recognized your own sailors this way? Sometimes getting even the smallest recognition goes a long way. I provided many positive counseling sheets to my sailors. Each one takes only a few minutes of your time, but your sailors won't take them for granted and will be grateful for your praise.

Sailor of the Quarter/Year

Have you ever been selected as Sailor of the Quarter or Sailor of the Year? If not, why not? This should be a goal you set for yourself. Is there so much competition at your command that you don't get selected from your department? Then you're not putting forth enough effort to be competitive. You must be willing to do more than your superiors expect of you.

Or do you believe you must play politics to get selected? Petty Officer Allen thought so, whereas Petty Officer Robbins made it one of his goals to be selected as his command's Sailor of the Year. Allen was never selected as, or even nominated for, Sailor of the Quarter, much less Sailor of the Year. He never set this as a goal to achieve—but you should. Being Sailor of the Quarter or Year isn't required to become a chief petty officer, but these recognitions represent valuable points you otherwise won't receive at the selection board. Our two first class petty officers are both outstanding at their jobs, but the Wheel of Success highlights the real differences between them. When you see how they stacked up against each other in terms of the points earned within each section of the Wheel, you'll see why one was selected. (Appendix II shows the points earned in each of the ten sections by Petty Officers Allen and Robbins.)

Similar to Sailor of the Quarter, have you ever nominated one of your sailors for Bluejacket or Junior Sailor of the Quarter/Year?

If not, why not? This is an aspect of leadership that will not only motivate your sailors but let them know you're taking care of them as well. Recognition is not only for you but for the sailors around you, too. If you've never set the goal of being selected as a Sailor of the Quarter or Year for yourself, then you probably don't feel such recognition is important for your sailors either. But you couldn't be more wrong. And if you do feel it's important for your sailors, then why not for yourself as well?

Special Assignments

Have you ever been on an Individual Augmentee, Global War on Terrorism Support Assignment, or Overseas Contingency Operation Support Assignment? Did you receive an award for your assignment? Just having one of these assignments on your record isn't enough. To be competitive among your peers, you need to stand out. If you volunteered for and completed one of these assignments yet did not receive an award, it begs the question "Why?" Even if you aren't recognized with an award—and sometimes this is the case—your evaluation should show that you did more than your job. If you're selected for one of these assignments, you *must* put forth the effort to stand out among those you're serving with. Only hard work will make you stand out; after all, if it were easy, everyone would do it. If you spend any extra time you may have while on assignment simply waiting around to come home, the chief petty officer selection board will notice. *Just doing your job is not enough.*

It matters which of these assignments you volunteer for; some are more career-enhancing than others. The assignments that stand out include Iraq, Afghanistan, the Horn of Africa, and Guantanamo Bay, Cuba. In contrast, volunteering for Kuwait is not going to be career-enhancing in comparison to someone who deploys to those other areas. The Global War on Terrorism is not currently being fought in Kuwait. But it may be again in the future; with the world changing, it's important to stay on top of world events and think about how they might affect the mission of the Navy both now and in the future.

Speak to your Command Individual Augmentee Coordinator to help clarify these matters. He or she will have more detailed information, including the current taskers, and can advise on which taskers would be more career-enhancing and make you stand out among your peers. Again, it's not about making someone else look bad, it's about presenting yourself as positively as possible before the chief petty officer selection board.

Volunteer Community Service Medal

Have you ever earned the Military Outstanding Volunteer Service Medal (MOVSM)? If not, why not? I will cover this subject in more detail in Chapter VIII, but until then suffice it to say that this medal represents a great opportunity to earn an award while performing valuable community service.

The key to earning the medal is consistency: volunteering for community service and events over a three-year period. The final authority for conferring an MOVSM is your commanding officer.

Higher Medals and End-of-Tour Awards

At any time during your career have you been awarded a NAM or higher, either during your tour or at the end? At this point in your career, I would hope so. Both are good, but earning a specific award during your tour at the command may be prized more highly than just an end-of-tour (EOT) award.

Some sailors feel they deserve an EOT award just because they're transferring. But simply doing your job and staying out of trouble do not justify an EOT award. There is a distinct difference between *earning* an award and being *given* an award. Just because you *feel* you *should* receive an award doesn't mean you've *earned* one. If a sailor is doing "just enough" to justify an EOT award, should he get one?

Such questions are not for me to decide; that's up to the command. If it conducts awards boards on a regular schedule, leading chief petty officers should be prepared to justify whether sailors in their departments deserve awards for specific achievements or upon completing their tours. Remember, when you're a chief, you'll be making decisions of this kind. So be a leader and take care of your sailors; if you don't, they'll notice.

Models and Examples

One sailor who was very good at recognizing his sailors was Command Master Chief Herbert Kelton. I met him while he was the command master chief at Naval Support Activity Lakehurst, New Jersey. He used several programs to recognize sailors for their actions.

The Navy Sailor of the Year program recognizes sailors for each quarter of the year as well as the year overall in Bluejacket, Junior, and Senior Sailor categories. Master Chief Kelton added to this the Command Master Chief "Picture of the Week." This program allowed sailors to stand out within their divisions or departments. While I was there, the program was in full force. Sailors would go out of their way to show their leaders why they should be selected to appear in the picture of the week. Upon selecting a sailor, Master Chief Kelton would take his or her picture and send it out to all hands. The picture would be accompanied by an explanation of what actions during the week got this sailor nominated by his or her chain of command and selected by the command master chief. At first glance, I thought this program was pretty trivial—until I saw the friendly competition that arose within the command and the camaraderie that came from being nominated and selected. I very quickly realized it was in fact a great program. Recognizing our sailors is never a trivial matter.

Another great program Command Master Chief Kelton put in place at the naval support activity was the "Hard Charger of the Week." Each department would recommend a sailor it felt deserved to be recognized for his or her actions during the week. Master Chief Kelton would write a letter to the family of the sailor selected explaining why their son or daughter was selected. Again, I saw first-hand how sailors competed against one another, yet the overall effect was to build camaraderie within the command.

Neither of these programs provided any formal Navy recognition to a sailor, but they did show sailors that their chain of command appreciated their contributions. Even recognition that doesn't fall into the "award" category can have a huge impact on sailors both professionally and personally. And when sailors are recognized instead of driven, it builds camaraderie within the command. Receiving appropriate recognition can have a lasting effect on the sailor, the command, and the Navy.

Robbins and Allen

Petty Officer Allen has earned three NAMs during his career (not counting his projected end-of-tour award, which he hasn't received yet). He completed an Individual Augmentee assignment in Kuwait, but received no award because he failed to perform above and beyond the call of duty. Petty Officer Allen was more interested in going home than doing his job, which resulted in a less-than-stellar Individual Augmentee assignment.

Petty Officer Robbins has earned an NCM, three NAMs—one for his Individual Augmentee assignment in Guantanamo Bay, Cuba—and the MOVSM. Unlike Petty Officer Allen, Petty Officer Robbins made the most of his assignment in Cuba and was rewarded for his performance.

Not every sailor in an Individual Augmentee, Global War on Terrorism Support, or Overseas Contingency Operation Support Assignment will receive an award. Awards should be earned. Setting a goal is one thing; it's quite another to put forth the hard work necessary to achieve it. If you don't make the effort to follow through, all you're doing is wasting the valuable time you need to set yourself up for success and make yourself more competitive among your peers.

Writing Awards

As a first class petty officer, you should be well-versed in the art of writing excellent evaluations and awards for both yourself and your sailors. Otherwise, you need to catch up quickly, because you're doing everybody a disservice.

If you're still struggling to write good awards for your sailors, go to your chief to get the benefits of his or her leadership experience. If any of your fellow first class petty officers write great awards, ask them for help. If you're not sure whether your write-up is "up to snuff," simply ask someone else to go through your award and see how it reads. There's absolutely no reason not to ask for help when you need it. If you feel you can't ask questions because it will undermine you as a leader or because you're simply above asking questions, rethink your attitude. (Don't forget to take a moment to spell-check your awards. If you route an award write-up containing spelling errors up your chain of command, it tells them you aren't taking it seriously enough.)

I've included examples at the end of this chapter of both good and bad award write-ups. If you're already a great award writer, you'll see the difference between the two awards right away. Both may initially look like good awards, but only one is actually well-written. The other is written to just sound good; it has none of the substance that would be useful to the chief petty officer selection board. Studying these two award examples can help you write better ones yourself. Put these award write-ups in your sailor toolbox for future reference.

That's good advice in general. Throughout my career I kept copies of the awards I wrote for my sailors. Sometimes you can pull good bullets from one and plug them into another. But be careful: the write-ups for your sailors should not all read the same. Awards should be unique to each situation, except when several sailors are being recognized for the same actions. If you use the same award over and over again, you're demonstrating no growth in your ability to write awards. It also dilutes the value of the award if your sailors hear the same write-up read at every award presentation.

Take the time to capture the intangibles that make the person and his or her actions worthy of being singled out for recognition, and put the information together in such a way that it flows well for the reader and the awardee. Be resourceful!

MA1 (SW/EXW) League from Mobile Security Squadron Two Detachment Two-three receives a Navy Commendation Medal while on deployment in Rota, Spain. Petty Officer League was selected to chief petty officer the following year. *James C. Glass*

FC1 (SW) Jasso from Naval Support Activity Lakehurst, New Jersey, receives a Navy Achievement Medal after being selected as the Senior Sailor of the Quarter. Petty Officer Jasso was selected as the Sailor of the Year for Naval Support Activity Lakehurst. *James C. Glass*

Sample Text for a Service Award - 1

(GOLD STAR IN LIEU OF SECOND AWARD)

MASTER-AT-ARMS FIRST CLASS (SURFACE WARFARE) JOHN DOE UNITED STATES NAVY.

PROFESSIONAL ACHIEVEMENT AS LEADING PETTY OFFICER FOR MOBILE SECURITY SQUADRON TWO, DETACHMENT TWO THREE FROM 21 JANUARY 2006 TO 15 JULY 2007. THROUGH HIS SUPERIOR LEADERSHIP ABILITIES, THE DETACHMENT EARNED AN OVERALL SCORE OF 94% DURING FEP, THE HIGHEST SCORE EARNED BY ANY DETACHMENT WITHIN NAVAL COASTAL WARFARE GROUP TWO. HE PLAYED A KEY ROLE IN THE LOGISTICS, PLANNING, AND TRAINING OF 18 MISSIONS CARRYING SEVERAL BILLION DOLLARS WORTH OF EQUIPMENT AND SUPPLIES TRANSITING THROUGHOUT THE 6TH FLEET AREA OF RESPONSIBILTY WITHOUT INCIDENT. HIS LEADERSHIP AND GUIDANCE ENABLED 24 PERSONNEL TO QUALIFY FOR THEIR EXPEDITIONARY WARFARE QUALIFICATION. PETTY OFFICER DOE'S INITIATIVE, PERSEVERANCE, AND LOYAL DEVOTION TO DUTY REFLECTED CREDIT UPON HIMSELF AND WERE IN KEEPING WITH THE HIGHEST TRADITIONS OF THE UNITED STATES NAVAL SERVICE.

                              30 July 2007
                              I. M. SAILOR
                              CAPT, U.S. Navy
                    Naval Coastal Warfare Group Two

Sample Text for a Service Award - 2

(GOLD STAR IN LIEU OF THIRD AWARD)

ENGINEMAN FIRST CLASS (SURFACE WARFARE) JOHN DOE UNITED
STATES NAVY.

PROFESSIONAL ACHIEVEMENT AS LEADING PETTY OFFICER FOR
NAVAL WEAPONS STATION YORKTOWN BOAT DIVISION FROM 11
FEBRUARY 2010 TO 11 AUGUST 2011.   PETTY OFFICER DOE'S
OUTSTANDING PERFORMANCES AS LEADING PETTY OFFICER DIRECTLY
ENSURED THE SAFE AND SUCCESSFUL EXECUTION OF ALL BOAT
OPERATIONS DURING WEAPONS ONLOAD EVOLUTIONS WITHOUT
INCIDENT. HE SINGLE HANDEDLY ESTABLISHED AND MAINTAINED AN
OPTAR BUDGET FOR THE DEPARTMENT ENSURING ALL REQUISITIONS
WERE APPROVED AND ACCOUNTED FOR ENSURING THE UTMOST
ACCURACY. HIS LEADERSHIP QUALITIES WERE A DIRECT REFLECTION
OF THE SUCCESS FOR THE ENTIRE DEPARTMENT. PETTY OFFICER DOE'S
INITIATIVE, PERSEVERANCE, AND LOYAL DEVOTION TO DUTY
REFLECTED CREDIT UPON HIMSELF AND WERE IN KEEPING WITH THE
HIGHEST TRADITIONS OF THE UNITED STATES NAVAL SERVICE.

31 August 2011
I. M. SAILOR
CAPT, U.S. Navy
Naval Weapons Station Yorktown

Chapter 7

Collateral Duties

Why Collateral Duties?

In addition to your primary responsibilities, your command may assign you some extra jobs as collateral duties. Some commands want petty officers to voluntarily take on these new duties rather than being "volun-told," so to speak. It's usually easier to fill these positions when sailors volunteer than when they're assigned to them by their chain of command.

But some sailors volunteer for a collateral duty just to add another bullet to their evaluation; they believe this is the way to be competitive. However, this usually means the sailor will be inactive in the role, and the collateral duty becomes a waste of time instead of a way to help sailors, the command, or both. The other problem is that the prominence of the role the sailor is supposed to be filling only makes his inaction more noticeable to people within the command.

Instead, every collateral duty should represent a way a sailor can go above and beyond the call of duty—it's an opportunity to shine. Taking on a collateral duty also demonstrates a sailor's ability to take on more responsibility, a key ingredient of the Wheel of Success that paves your road toward becoming a chief petty officer. Successfully juggling your collateral duties alongside your normal assigned duties is a great way to showcase your abilities as a capable, responsible leader. If you can't yet do this, work on it. Just as becoming a leader doesn't happen overnight, being able to adapt to doing more than one thing at a time also takes hard work and dedication.

Although the term "collateral" means "secondary or subordinate," these duties are not unimportant. Yes, these duties can enhance your evaluations, but your goal in taking them on should be to perform them to the best of your ability. If you take on a collateral duty just to check another box on your evaluation, you're taking an opportunity away from someone who wants to demonstrate that he or she can take on more responsibility. It also hurts the sailors whom the collateral duty is intended to help. Anyone who is in a collateral duty role has a responsibility to make sure that it benefits sailors.

Your performance of collateral duties will be reflected in your evaluations—but not automatically in a good way. If you're unable to perform a collateral duty, your chain of command should realize this and not include it on your evaluation. And if you're able to perform the collateral duty but don't, I guarantee your chain of command will take notice, and this will be reflected in your evaluation. The tell-tale sign is when a collateral duty is listed in block 29 but nothing is written about it in block 43. When the chief petty officer selection board reads this, it will know there was no substance to your collateral duty, that you took it on for evaluation purposes only. An example would be claiming membership on the Diversity Committee but no events are listed in block 43. Months come and go without any fundraisers, lectures, or guest speakers relating to African American Month or Hispanic Heritage Month. The conclusion will be that you did not take the collateral duty seriously.

On the other hand, when you do a great job performing a collateral duty in addition to your normal duties, both sailors and your chain of command will take notice. This is especially true of high-visibility collateral duties. You should be able to capture these collateral duties in your brag sheet, and when you do a great job it should be reflected in your evaluations.

(By the way, you should update your brag sheet on a regular basis so you'll know exactly what you've accomplished within the evaluation cycle, instead of trying to recall all your accomplishments at the end. Remember, it's your career; don't expect your chain of command to recall your accomplishments for you—they already have a lot on their plates with evaluations, awards, inspections, etc. If you don't take your career seriously, why should anyone else?)

First class petty officers always seem to want to volunteer for collateral duties right after they've signed their evaluations. They suddenly want to work harder to improve their evaluations to be more competitive—or they just want some additional duties to appease the chain of command, to make everyone think they're doing more than they actually are. Does this sound like you? Has it worked for you? If you're wondering why not, have a heart-to-heart talk with your chiefs. They'll help you get back on the right track—the path to success instead of failure.

Primary and Collateral Duties

However, don't allow your collateral duties to become paramount—the only duties you take seriously. You can't afford to let your primary duties go unaccomplished. You must maintain a manageable balance between your varied and sometimes conflicting primary and collateral responsibilities. There's no shame in asking for help or guidance—everyone needs it from time to time—so don't be afraid to ask. Even as a chief petty officer, right on up to master chief, I didn't let my ego get in the way of getting the job done. I kept my feet planted on the ground, never forgetting where I came from. I was once in your shoes, and so were the other members of the chiefs' mess. Ask for help.

When I was a first class petty officer, I volunteered for several collateral duties, including key collateral duties within the command, because I felt that I was ready to assume greater responsibility. I also wanted to prove that I could do them all well.

However, an additional reason I ended up with so many collateral duties was because too few other sailors on the ship saw that taking on these extra responsibilities would be good for their career development—and their evaluations. (Again, don't take on a collateral duty just to pad your evaluation; it's performing a collateral duty *well* that will add to your evaluation.)

At one point I had taken on so many collateral duties that I was referred to as the "Command Collateral Duty Petty Officer." Having so many collateral duties was taking away from other parts of my job. Allowing this to happen will look bad at the chief petty officer selection board. You should be able to show an even flow of your accomplishments across the board instead of one area taking up most of your time. An example would be attempting to be almost a full-time student in pursuit of your degree instead of taking one or two classes per semester and putting similar time and energy into other areas, such as watch qualifications, community service, and diversity.

In my case, a chief petty officer stepped in to make sure my plate wasn't running over. He held a meeting of the chiefs' mess on why other sailors weren't taking on some of the collateral duties. The chief laid out his arguments and let it be known what he thought should be done. The command master chief held a meeting with the first class petty officers and shared the chiefs' mess' thoughts. He stressed the importance of taking on more responsibility and how sailors need to work together to achieve a common goal. In the end, some of my collateral duties were spun off to other first class petty officers who had decided they wanted more responsibility and an opportunity to showcase their potential.

Diving In

Collateral duties are not required of any first class petty officer, unless directed by authority. But taking on collateral duties can benefit you in your career, setting you up for success in several ways. They teach you additional skills, demonstrate your leadership qualities, and make you stand out from your peers. There are many types of collateral duties a first class petty officer can take on that will carry weight at the chief petty officer selection board—as long as you take them seriously and put in enough time to do them well. That way you'll be able to document on paper that what you did had substance and was constructive.

For example, say you volunteered to be the Command Combined Federal Campaign Coordinator. During the campaign you made contact with everyone in the command, 100 percent. Your command's goal was to raise $7,000, and you were able to raise $9,200. Maybe you accomplished these results through fundraisers, command events, or other methods. You obviously performed this collateral duty very well. Or, say you contacted everyone but raised only $6,000. Even though you didn't reach the monetary goal, it wouldn't necessarily mean you didn't perform the collateral duty well; after all, you can't control how much someone donates, and any money raised is better than nothing.

Command collateral duties carry more points than departmental ones, and will always have more impact on the selection board. But your performance of both command and departmental collateral duties can demonstrate command impact. You should also understand that some "collateral" duties will not gain you any extra points at the board because they're considered to be an integral part of your rating. For example, a master-at-arms who serves as the Command Urinalysis Coordinator gains no points because knowing how to perform these duties is part of his or her rate. Such a first class petty officer would benefit from volunteering for a different collateral duty.

Doing the Right Thing for the Right Reason

The purpose of most collateral duties is to provide guidance and information to sailors about matters that affect them both as individual citizens and as members of the military. Collateral duties play an integral part within any command structure, whether they're specific to a department or apply to the whole command. What difference does it make whether someone does them well or badly?

Consider the Command Financial Specialist—you. A sailor comes to you for advice. But let's say you took on this role only because it would pad your evaluation, not to help sailors. When this sailor seeks your assistance with a troubled financial situation, the "advice" you provide not only doesn't help him, it pushes him into even worse financial turmoil. Now, let's say you do the same with twenty more sailors who come to you for advice. At this point the command may have a problem, because if these sailors are unable to resolve their financial woes, they may end up losing their security clearances—with drastic ramifications. The sailors may be discharged if they can neither get their clearances back nor cross over to a rating that doesn't require one. And what happens if one of these sailors is required to deploy as an Individual Augmentee, which usually requires a security clearance? More than likely he or she will be discharged.

Although this is just one example, I hope it makes clear that not performing a collateral duty to the best of your ability can have ramifications for you, the sailors with whom you serve, and your command, including trickle-down effects you may not even anticipate.

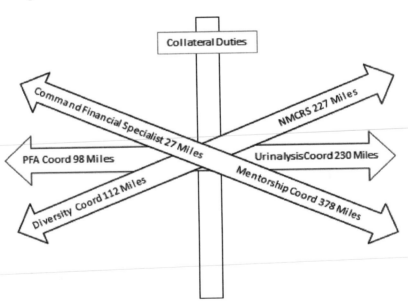

Make sure you have a handle on the collateral duties assigned to you—not the other way around. If you take on too many additional collateral duties you may find yourself lost, looking up at the road sign, deciding which direction to turn.

Chapter 8

Command Involvement

The First Class Petty Officers' Association

As a first class petty officer, you should be actively involved within your command. One of the simplest vehicles for doing so is the command's First Class Petty Officers' Association (FCPOA). Although the FCPOA has overall bylaws, each association is unique to its command. The FCPOA can provide a positive impact for sailors and the community by being actively involved both on and off the command.

If you are a member of the Association who volunteers his time at functions such as coat drives, holiday food drives, command picnics, Navy ball fundraisers, and MWR events, those are all good deeds. But if you're that actively involved, you should hold an office. Become the president, vice president, or treasurer. This will help to show your leadership potential. In contrast, if you're a member or even have one of these titles, but play no active role in this capacity, the chief petty officer selection board will look at this as nothing at all. Let's say you're the president of the association. If you do play an active role, you must have done something tangible for which you can be recognized for your efforts; otherwise, don't waste your time, or the selection board's time, in mentioning it. These tangible markers might include numbers of dollars the Association raised through various fundraisers, hours contributed toward special events such as food drives or highway adoptions, or personnel who volunteered for the association or who received donations from the association.

Each of our first class petty officers is president of the FCPOA at his command. But look closely at their evaluations; note that the office adds nothing tangible to Petty Officer Allen's evaluation, whereas YN1 Robbins plays an active role as president of his Association, and that's reflected in his evaluation. The selection board will notice the difference.

Training and Inspections

The active role the FCPOA can play is not limited to its impact on the community beyond the command. Enlisted sailors within the command benefit when the FCPOA conducts advancement training, warfare training, or specialized training such as that for a Damage Control Training Team member or Combat System Training Team member. When FCPOA members play an active role by organizing such training, it provides the benefit of their collective experience to other sailors.

First class petty officers are experts within their rates who should be committed to training their sailors. As qualified warfare specialists, what you already know can be critical to the success of the sailors around you. You are the Navy's first-line leaders; you possess the knowledge and experience to train those around you, which builds the foundation for consistent mission accomplishment. Share this knowledge—don't keep it a secret! Inaction in this area may cause your sailors to avoid you rather than respect you.

Your knowledge can be instrumental to command mission success when it comes to inspections. Are you playing a positive role in command inspections, such as the ones listed below?

1. Inspection & survey (INSURV)

2. Unit-level training (ULTRA)

3. Final evaluation problem (FEP)

4. Hurricane exercise (HURREX)

5. Tactical readiness evaluation (TRE)

6. Operational reactor safeguard exam (ORSE)

7. Pre-overseas movement certification (POMCERT)

8. Nuclear weapons technical inspection (NWTI)

9. Supply management inspection (SMI)

10. Conventional ordnance safety review (COSR)

If your command is unable to achieve a passing score on these inspections, that has a significant impact on mission readiness. Contributing to your command passing these inspections is a great way for you to get involved. Playing a key role is even better, because it shows the chief petty officer selection board your leadership potential and breaks you out from among your peers. Hard work and dedication form the foundation of good leadership.

Chapter 9

Community Involvement

Community Involvement and the Wheel

The purpose of the Wheel of Success is to provide you with a well-balanced set of tools for success. Community involvement is one component of the Wheel. The details of how you proceed in this area are up to you.

There are countless community projects you could volunteer for: adopt-a-highway, adopt-a-school, food drives, coat drives, boys and girls clubs, or the parent-teacher association, among many others. Active membership is crucial. For example, if you're a member of the parent-teacher association, you would provide active support through assisting with fundraisers, book drives, tutoring, etc. These opportunities offer many good ways of being recognized by the community, most commonly by letters of appreciation or commendation.

Making the Most of Volunteering

Community involvement is a great way to become engaged and demonstrate your leadership potential. Acting on your Navy Pride demonstrates your ability to build and foster community relationships. Volunteering your time showcases your support for the community—and performing a great service for the community also feels good!

While participation is good, taking on a leadership role is even better. For example, if you volunteered for a community project such as Habitat for Humanity and provided eight hours of your time installing windows, this would be a great way to support your community. But if you took a leading role on the same project by recruiting fifteen other volunteers from the command to assist with grounds maintenance, plumbing, and installing windows over an eight-hour period, not only would you have contributed your own time but you also would have demonstrated your leadership ability by leveraging your time into 120 additional man-hours supporting the project (eight hours times 15 volunteers). You don't need to take the lead on every community project, but consistency is the key to success.

Imaginative Applications

While I was in Iraq the first time, in 2004, I was selected as a chief petty officer. Three other first class petty officers in the area were selected as well. As part of the transition process, we were charged with making some sort of contribution to the community. But we were limited in our options because some of the typical forms of community involvement, such as adopt-a-highway or "Earth Day Beautification," were simply nonapplicable in the middle of an armed conflict. Still, we wanted to do something as a group, so the four of us got together and began brainstorming ideas.

Finally we came up with "Operation Bright Smile." We thought it would definitely help the community. We would collect toothpaste, toothbrushes, and dental floss and provide training to the Iraqis on dental hygiene. Although we ourselves weren't permitted to go off base to teach the locals, the members of the American military medical and dental staffs assigned to train the local hospitals and medical facilities were permitted to do so. Whenever they went out, they took the items we'd collected with them and taught the locals how to use them to improve dental hygiene. The medical and dental staffs found that the Iraqis knew little about basic dental hygiene but were more than willing to learn. The Iraqi children were the most willing to learn; to them, learning anything new was fun, including about dental hygiene.

During the six weeks we were there we collected more than ten thousand toothbrushes, tubes of toothpaste, and containers of dental floss. In fact, Operation Bright Smile was such a huge success that it continued even after we completed our tours.

Community Involvement for its Own Sake— A Brief Reminder

Although my comrades and I received no formal awards for Operation Bright Smile, we were proud to be doing something good—the satisfaction we received from performing a great service to the Iraqis was reward enough. It wasn't about us, it was about helping others. In general, getting involved in the community can bring many intangible rewards, and you don't always have to get recognition for your efforts.

The Military Outstanding Volunteer Service Medal (MOVSM)

However, for those sailors who go above and beyond the call of duty in community involvement, formal Navy recognition is available. You may be eligible for the MOVSM. This is a great reward for a job well done.

I previously discussed this medal in Chapter VI: Awards. Have you ever earned this medal? If you volunteer your time over a three-year period, you may qualify. If you demonstrate that you meet the requirements, your commanding officer has the authority to approve you for the medal. (I provide an example of a write-up for the medal below.) It shows you the kind of information needed to qualify. You may realize you've already made yourself eligible without knowing it. Your Administration Department can also assist you in completing a write-up for the medal, including providing examples. Keeping example award write-ups always enabled me to write awards in less time while also being more creative.

From: Commanding Officer, Naval Support Activity, Lakehurst
To: OS1 (SW/AW) John P. Jones, USN, XXX-XX-6789

Subj: AWARD OF THE MILITARY OUTSTANDING VOLUNTEER SERVICE MEDAL

Ref: (a) SECNAVINST 1650.1G

1. In accordance with reference (a), you are hereby authorized to wear the Military Outstanding Volunteer Service Medal for outstanding public service with Big Brothers/Big Sisters of Ocean County from September 2008 to June 2009; National Education Association's "Read Across America" Program from September 2008 to July 2011; "Thanksgiving Food Basket Program" during November 2008, 2009, 2010; Navy Ball Committee from March 2009 to March 2010; Second Class Petty Officers Association Multiple Sclerosis Walk 2010 and 2011; Naval Support Activity's Travel and Leisure Show during April 2011; Navy and Marine Corps Relief Society from March 2010 to May 2010 and Naval Support Activity's Youth Activity Center from September 2008 to July 2011.

2. As a direct representative of the Command and the Navy, you gave many hours to the families of Navy Lakehurst through your tireless efforts in ensuring Thanksgiving meals for those in need. Your untiring selfless devotion played an integral part in raising over $15k for the Navy and Marine Corps Relief Society. Your leadership allowed you to positively affect the lives of many when you devoted your time to the Bergen County Rape Crisis Center. Additionally, you actively participated in the Earth Day Beautification Project during the past year, which proved instrumental in aesthetically improving the base. Also, between 2010 and 2011, you helped collect and discard 3,420 pounds of refuse from three miles of local highways. Your initiative provided clean roadways and helped beautify the community.

3. Your tireless efforts and exceptional dedication in supporting your community and youth brought about a sense of "Unity in the Community" within the command, in addition to surrounding neighborhoods. You were inspirational in making a difference in the lives of those less fortunate and the youth in the community. Your service is a direct reflection of the best attributes of our Navy and nation. Because of your professionalism, initiative, and loyal devotion to serve the public, you reflected great credit upon yourself and the United States Naval Service.

4. Congratulations on a service well done!

C. O. OFFICER

Earning this medal can provide a big boost at the chief petty officer selection board. It sends a positive statement to the board that you have been consistent in volunteering your time to the community. This gives you an advantage over someone without the medal, and an even greater advantage over your peers who don't volunteer for community projects at all. For whatever reason, they've decided to spend their time elsewhere; they may believe that being the best in their rate, by itself, will ensure them promotion to chief petty officer. Whatever the reason, you will have demonstrated an ability to maximize an opportunity they failed to take advantage of.

Robbins and Allen

Both YN1 Allen and YN1 Robbins volunteered their time to community projects. However, Petty Officer Allen decided his time was too valuable for any deeper community involvement. Petty Officer Robbins, on the other hand, found time to volunteer to lead a community project. As First Class Petty Officer Association president, he showcased his ability as a leader by raising over $3,000 in various fundraisers for the Navy Ball. He also coordinated and led 36 sailors who provided over 280 man-hours to refurbishing a local public school, saving the community over $10,000 in commercial contracts and equipment. In volunteering his time to community projects, Petty Officer Robbins qualified for and earned his MOVSM.

When going before the chief petty officer selection board, would you rather show the record of community involvement of Robbins or Allen? Are you willing to put in the time and hard work to make that happen?

Chapter 10

Diversity

What Does Diversity Mean?

Although the term "diversity" is generally used to refer to matters of equal opportunity with regard to race, gender, culture, religion, and ethnicity, as used in the Wheel of Success the term refers to the diverse roles of a sailor.

The Wheel of Success illustrates why having diversity amongst your roles and assignments makes you more competitive among your peers. Numerous duty assignments can help with this, but you have to know which ones. As usual, talking with your chiefs and having a career development board can help you find out.

No matter what your current duty station or your primary duty assignment is, it provides you with opportunities to excel, and you must take advantage of them. That sort of excellence in performance is what separates those sailors who rise above their contemporaries from those left wondering why they're not advancing. Just having an assignment, even one that adds diversity, does nothing for you if all you do is show up. Just like most other aspects of your career that we've discussed, thinking of diversity as just "a check in the box" will have no positive impact on you, your evaluation, or the chief petty officer selection board. You must use the assignment to become more competitive—make the most of every tour.

Particular Duties

Some duties that provide diversity are serving as a recruiter, recruit trainer, or instructor.

Serving as a recruiter involves interacting with the community while promoting the Navy as a potential job or career. Recruiters shape the future of our Navy and our country by enlisting civilians to become a part of the Navy. With the ever-increasing technological sophistication of our Navy ships, submarines, and aircraft, recruiting the best and brightest young men and women to serve is ever more important. If you're able to not only function but thrive in this kind of environment, it will certainly make you more competitive among your peers—especially in comparison to any sailor who signed up to be a recruiter but did not make a success of it.

Another similarly valuable diversity assignment is being a recruit division commander. Not only is this a challenging assignment, but it gives you the chance to mold the future of the Navy, in the form of its newest sailors. You set the tone for them as a role model and mentor, and make a difference in their lives. In this assignment you can earn the Military Training Specialist qualification. A successful assignment as a recruit division commander displays your leadership qualities, which will pay huge dividends at the chief petty officer selection board.

Instructor duty can be challenging yet very rewarding; the opportunity to teach sailors is a gift. However, while you're assigned to instructor duty you *must* also earn your Military Training Specialist qualification. If you don't, you're telling the chief petty officer selection board that the unique opportunity you received wasn't important to you—and the board will see it the same way.

Special Overseas Assignments

An Individual Augmentee or Overseas Support Assignment constitutes a diversity assignment that gives you a great opportunity to show your leadership capabilities. The Global War on Terrorism has provided a number of such opportunities for sailors to volunteer for assignment to Iraq, Afghanistan, Kuwait, the Horn of Africa, and Guantanamo Bay, Cuba.

Although each of these assignments has a unique mission, some are more career-enhancing than others; contact your Command Individual Augmentee Coordinator or your detailer for more information. If selected for one of these assignments, make sure you have a productive tour. This doesn't necessarily mean you must receive an award—although receiving one is great. But you must have played an integral part in the success of the mission. If this is not mentioned in an award, it must be stated in your evaluation.

Petty Officers Allen and Robbins both volunteered for and served Individual Augmentee or Overseas Support Assignment tours of duty. But Petty Officer Allen thought of his Individual Augmentee assignment as just a check in the box, and was more focused on getting back home than on taking advantage of the opportunity. Plus, his chosen assignment, in Kuwait, was not very career-enhancing—which he would have known ahead of time if he had contacted the Command Individual Augmentee Coordinator or requested a career development board. In contrast, Petty Officer Robbins volunteered for two Individual Augmentee Assignments, in Iraq and in Guantanamo Bay, Cuba, and was awarded for doing a great job—going above and beyond the call of duty.

Navy Community Diversity

Taking on challenges both at sea and ashore will also showcase your abilities in diverse venues. Successfully taking on challenging assignments onboard ships, in submarines, on aircraft, overseas, or in independent duty situations gives you the opportunity to display adaptability. Such assignments provide great opportunities to set and achieve specific goals and excel while doing so. Serving in a DDG, then in a CVN will not only diversify you but provide opportunities to excel as a leader. This is especially true if you become a leading petty officer at sea—demonstrated capacity to answer this leadership challenge makes the biggest possible impression on a chief petty officer selection board.

Occasionally, someone has to do back-to-back shore tours because of his or her particular rating, or the need may be Navy Enlisted Classification driven. If you find yourself in this situation, do something with it! This is when you need to produce in the areas of continuing education, community involvement, command collateral duties, command involvement, etc. If you don't, you're shooting yourself in the foot. Whatever your assignment, there's always something you can do to make yourself more competitive. If you don't know what it is, ask your chief.

Back-to-back type 3 duty may not help you. Some sailors feel it's career-enhancing, but it could prove to be counterproductive. A sailor who does a shore tour in Japan, followed by serving in a ship based in Japan, followed by another shore tour or neutral duty in Japan, stays in the same geographical area and gains no additional credit for taking the "hard job" overseas. While this may not hurt you, the chief petty officer selection board may decide that by staying overseas you robbed another sailor of the chance to diversify himself. Try to be more diverse.

Taking the Hard Look

After I was selected to chief petty officer, I sat down with my mentor to begin looking at what I needed to achieve to be more competitive among my peers and be selected to senior chief petty officer. I had an idea of what my new goals should be—but knowing is always better than guessing. After a few hours of looking in my record at what I had already achieved, my mentor informed me of some directions I should go to break out from among my peers.

I didn't like what he had written down—but I now know that he set me up for success. Sometimes making yourself more competitive means taking on the hard assignments, working hard to do them very well—and then turning right around and setting new, hard goals to achieve. I had set some goals for myself in advance, but it was the goals my mentor and I together set for me that helped me succeed at becoming a senior chief petty officer. In fact, I was selected to senior chief petty officer the first time I was board-eligible. Furthermore, after I was selected to senior chief petty officer, I again met with my mentor and set new goals for myself. These goals set me up for success again: I was selected to master chief petty officer the first time I was board-eligible, as well.

Diversity in Advice

The advice I received from my many mentors throughout my career was very helpful, not only for myself but also in mentoring other sailors. An ability to learn from others, adapt what you've learned, and develop and use many traits is part of successful leadership—and diversity contributes to all of them.

Like any of the ten areas of the Wheel of Success, you need to strike a balance between diversity and the others. You can do more in one area than another—in fact, your service community may require it—but you should practice an essential balance. If you have any questions, speak to your chiefs or have a career development board. This will clarify not only for the chiefs but for yourself where you stand on your goals: which ones have been achieved, and which ones you may need to change. Yes, it's your career, but there's nothing wrong with asking questions or getting help.

You need to get yourself on the right path. While you may feel a goal would be a good one to achieve, it may not help you become a chief petty officer. Some goals you may want to achieve anyway, just because they're important to you. But, in the interests of your success, don't let them distract you from focusing on the goals and areas that make you more competitive.

Chapter 11

Education

Opportunities and Balance

Education is a very easy way to become more competitive among your peers. It can take many forms, including completing correspondence courses, taking individual college courses, earning a degree, or participating in the United States Military Apprenticeship Program.

Just remember, when you're deciding how to use your time: if you don't become chief petty officer board-eligible, nothing else matters—your record will never be seen by the board. And until you pass the E-7 test, you can't become board-eligible. So, while education is important, studying for the chief's exam is a must. Although applying the Wheel of Success can help you become competitive among your peers, studying for your exam and becoming board-eligible needs to be your priority. Otherwise, the board may never see the best candidate—which might have been you. On the other hand, someone else took the time to study and you didn't—so maybe you weren't the best candidate after all. Study, study, study.

Of all the educational possibilities listed above, earning a college degree carries the most weight. While simply receiving college credits for completing courses is good, earning a degree is significantly better. Not only does it make you more competitive among your peers, it also makes you more marketable in your post-Navy career. Luckily, completing a college degree while still in the Navy is easier than ever before. Tuition assistance pays one hundred percent of your tuition, and sailors can take college classes leading to associate's, bachelor's, master's, and even doctoral degrees. Sailors benefit from a great program without having to pay money out of their own pockets. If you haven't already started a degree program, look into it very seriously.

However, to reiterate an earlier reminder: be careful not to overload yourself with too many educational commitments, to the point where they interfere with performing your normal duties. You need to strike the balance at which you're competitive among your peers and not focusing too much in one area. You must ensure you're doing your best in an area, but not to the point where it interferes with your job, your other assigned duties, or even with mission readiness. By keeping your goals in balance, you'll find a good equilibrium in your professional and personal life.

What to Study?

When setting your goal, don't just pick the level of degree you want to earn (associate's, bachelor's etc.); have a degree plan in place as well. If you just start taking courses and aren't sure what you want your degree to be in, you could be taking classes you won't need, which means you'll take longer than necessary to earn a degree.

In deciding what degree is best for you, look at the bigger picture. If you're a master-at-arms, getting a degree in Criminal Justice may be the best choice. However, if you aren't going to pursue a career in that field once you transition from the Navy into the civilian world, it may benefit you more to get a degree in your targeted field.

Although I was a master-at-arms for many years, when I made the transition to command master chief I sat down with my academic counselor. He advised me to go in a different direction than a degree in Criminal Justice. After looking at the options, I decided that a degree in Applied Management would benefit me more after I retired from the Navy. This ended up being the right decision for me. It might not be for you, but always keep your options open.

The United States Military Apprenticeship Program

This program offers an array of apprenticeship programs for each rating. Although it doesn't yield a college degree, it allows sailors to develop specialties within their ratings. For example, a master-at-arms can fulfill an apprenticeship as a dispatcher or as a police officer.

Within the Navy, earning a United States Military Apprenticeship will help make you more competitive among your peers for advancement. If you get out of the Navy to pursue a civilian job, apprenticeships can figure prominently in your résumé.

As a first class petty officer, if you practice what you preach to your sailors and complete an apprenticeship program, it shows the chief petty officer selection board that you're serious about furthering your education. For board purposes, an apprenticeship earns you approximately the same number of points as an associate's degree. So earning an associate's degree as well as an apprenticeship puts you one up on your peers who earn just an associate's degree.

Correspondence Courses

Numerous correspondence courses from a wide range of programs are available to sailors. Correspondence courses can be completed anytime during the year, and each sailor should try to complete at least one correspondence course per year.

The good thing about correspondence courses is they're easily accessible. And there's nothing wrong with completing a particular correspondence course just because it piques your interest. But sailors should know which ones are beneficial to their careers; consult your chain of command or command career counselor if you have any questions.

Any courses required for training, such as annual General Military Training courses, are not credited as correspondence courses that add points at the chief petty officer selection board, since all sailors are required to complete them. Also, before you take correspondence courses that are out of your rating, get guidance from your chief. The selection board may not believe these to be worth any extra points. Although you may decide to complete them anyway, to make chief you should complete correspondence courses that break you out from among your peers.

Robbins and Allen

YN1 Allen has never taken any college courses, but completed the United States Military Apprenticeship Program for his rating. He also completed several correspondence courses and Navy Knowledge Online (NKO) courses outside of his rating.

YN1 Robbins earned his bachelor's degree and has completed two courses toward his master's degree. Like Allen, he completed several correspondence courses and NKO courses outside his rating.

Thus, both petty officers completed some of the areas in the education sector of the Wheel of Success. Although Petty Officer Robbins earned his bachelor's degree, Petty Officer Allen focused sufficiently to earn a Military Apprenticeship Program within his rating.

Chapter 12

Sailorization

The Importance of Sailorization

Do you know what sailorization is? If you were new to the Navy I could understand if you were unfamiliar with this term, but as a first class petty officer you should not only be familiar with the term but be instrumental in sailorization.

Although sailorization begins at boot camp, it's a process that continues beyond boot camp graduation. First class petty officers should play an integral role in the personal and professional development of junior sailors, providing advice, training, counseling, mentorship, and positive role models. By doing so you reinforce the professional foundation these young sailors gained at Recruit Training Command, helping ready them to assume greater responsibility as their careers evolve.

Being involved with your sailors contributes both to their success and yours. It's up to you to help mold the minds of these up-and-coming leaders who will one day replace you, just as it's up to chief petty officers to mold the minds of their sailors who will one day replace them in the chiefs' mess. This is our job; if we can't do this, it's time to retire and let someone else do it. Being a leader is not a part-time job.

Through sailorization you enable the development of junior sailors and the continuation of their service. Your involvement, or lack thereof, may be the deciding factor in a sailor's success, or lack thereof, in and out of the Navy.

How Involved?

Practicing intrusive leadership demonstrates to your sailors that they're valued and appreciated, and that you desire to see them succeed. But intrusive leadership is not the same as micromanagement.

Let's say you're walking down the passageway of your ship and hear a couple of sailors talking to another sailor who will be turning 21 in two days about their plans to take him out to bars to celebrate his birthday. In your role as a leader, you speak to the sailors about drinking responsibly, remind them not to drive if they drink, and give them your off-duty phone number. You let them know that if they can't get a designated driver, they should call you for a safe ride back to the ship.

That's sound intrusive leadership, not unnecessary micro-management.

Retention

Positive retention results for your sailors can show your influence as a leader. As a first class petty officer, you have great potential to influence the sailors who work for you, and oftentimes those who don't as well.

However, some factors, both positive and negative, are beyond your control. Sailors who receive a selective reenlistment bonus are usually easier to retain in the Navy because they receive cash for reenlisting. On the other hand, some sailors are inclined to leave the Navy for a variety of reasons that may be nonnegotiable: they may want to see their family every night or go to college full time.

But others want to leave because they feel they're not being utilized to their full potential or they had a bad experience at their current or a previous command, and it's with sailors like these that you show your true impact as a leader and mentor. Use your influence to convince them of their true potential as future leaders of the Navy. If a sailor had a bad experience at the command, take the time to find out what it was. Communication is vital, but a sailor may not really be asking you to provide answers; sometimes what you need to do is listen, not speak. Sometimes that listening can make the difference between a sailor staying in the Navy or getting out.

Recognition

As part of sailorization, taking care of your sailors should be on your mind every day you come to work. One way to take care of your sailors is through awards—sailors love to be recognized. If sailors know their contributions are appreciated, they'll move mountains to get the job done for you.

Sailors can be recognized for their contributions to the community. The Military Outstanding Volunteer Service Medal is one of the easiest ways to get our sailors recognized. (See earlier discussion of this medal in Chapters VI and IX.) Commanding officers have the authority to confer this award on their sailors for sustained volunteer service to the community. All too often sailors who are volunteering for community service are unaware of the standards for receiving the medal. Some sailors may come very close to qualifying or even meet the standards yet be unaware of their status. Helping your sailors gain this recognition can be a relatively easy way you can make a difference.

The Sailor of the Quarter/Year Program is another great way to get your sailors recognized for their actions, but I believe it's one of the most underutilized programs in the Navy. There are great sailors out there who should be recognized and given the opportunity to represent their departments, and we are failing as leaders if we don't utilize the program fully. I've been at commands where this program was not taken seriously, with governing instructions that were either outdated or nonexistent. At these commands, I've immediately worked to get the program running at its full potential. Later, as a command master chief, I made it clear to the chiefs that if they had no representative from their departments, what did that say about their own ability to lead their sailors? As first class petty officers, not yet chiefs, you may find it easier to be complacent—but don't. Be active in the command; otherwise, you're part of the problem instead of the solution. Never be the sailor who utters the words, "This is the way we've always done it."

You don't need to wait until a sailor is transferring to initiate some sort of recognition—if this is the standard in place, it too represents a failure on our part as leaders. If sailors are doing great things at any time, they deserve support from their chain of command for suitable recognition. Not every sailor deserves an award—it can become diluted and lose its meaning. But when a sailor does receive recognition, it should happen in public, for everyone to witness.

Forms of recognition for accomplishments include mid-tour awards, letters of commendation or appreciation, "Division in the Spotlight" treatment, and publicizing in the plan of the day/week and base publications. Don't forget about the sailor's hometown newspaper or the possibility of a letter to his or her family describing the great job he or she is doing for the Navy. These latter examples are a good reminder that not all recognition needs to be in the form of an award. Praising a sailor at quarters or providing a positive counseling chit shows the division's, department's, or command's appreciation for hard work.

Recognition as an aspect of taking care of sailors is a vital role that leaders should never take lightly. Be a positive role model—lead by example.

Sailorization and Evaluations

Sailorization is incredibly important in today's fast-paced Navy: we all need to keep bringing our newer sailors along as quickly as possible. We build and lead sailors through retention, qualifications, advancement, education—all of which allow you to show your leadership. If you're not presently involved with your sailors in this way, talk to your chiefs about it!

It's amazing how many first class petty officers do make the effort to build their sailors, yet fail to put anything in their evaluations to reflect what they're doing. Excelling in this area as a first class petty officer can showcase your potential as a leader. Yes, sailorization is only one part of your job, and only one area of the Wheel of Success—but your performance at sailorization could make the difference between being selected or not at the chief petty officer selection board.

Are you up to the challenge? Reach out and touch sailors who want to be the best. If you end up with sailors beating down your door because of what you can pass on to them, it's a sign you're becoming a great leader and mentor—and you'll be well on your way to becoming a chief petty officer.

Chapter 13

Warfare, Special, and Watch Qualifications

The Importance of Qualifications

Today's Navy operates in an environment that requires every enlisted service member to have a basic understanding of the different platforms they're assigned to. It's imperative for sailors to qualify for the specific warfare programs in the various communities they're attached to. When sailors have a higher level of understanding and working knowledge of the platforms to which they're assigned, it increases mission readiness and amplifies the overall success of the command.

Some qualifications, such as those for submarine warfare, have been mandatory for years. Other than such cases, however, it used to be that sailors who earned warfare qualifications did so because they wanted to stand out and be more competitive among their peers. Until 2010, earning a warfare qualification where it was available was required only for second class petty officers and above. However, in 2010 the master chief petty officer of the Navy made it a requirement for every sailor. Since all warfare qualifications are now mandatory, this is one less area by which you can break out from among your peers. Qualifications are still part of the Wheel of Success, but paying attention to all the areas of the Wheel so as to become a well-rounded sailor is even more important to fulfilling your goal of becoming a chief petty officer.

While the command expects you to achieve the applicable warfare qualification during your tour of duty, each one actually has its own different but defined timeline allotted to earning it. This is what you should set as your goal. Amongst all of the other qualifications a sailor must attain, this one should be automatic for every one of you.

It's vital that you understand the importance of the warfare program and the significant ramifications a failure to earn one can have on your career. Failure to achieve the qualification during the designated period could have lasting, even devastating effects on your career. The Navy is downsizing, and it could decide it no longer needs your services.

I still come in contact with first class petty officers who didn't take advantage of their opportunity—and now it has come back to haunt them. While formerly the command could allow a first class petty officer to take the chief petty officer test even if he had the opportunity to earn a warfare designation but didn't, this is no longer the case. If you don't earn your warfare qualification when you have the opportunity, your chances of being selected to chief will be even slimmer than before, perhaps nonexistent.

New sailors may find completing the warfare designation difficult because it must be accomplished on top of on-the-job qualifications. Your chain of command should be instrumental in getting you on the right track, setting you up for success instead of failure. After all, you'll play an integral part in your division, department, and command.

Types of Qualifications

Of the many types of warfare qualifications in the Navy, some of the more common are represented by the Enlisted Surface Warfare Specialist, Enlisted Aviation Warfare Specialist, Submarine Warfare, and Seabee Combat Warfare devices. But not all commands are eligible to have a warfare qualification program in place.

Robbins and Allen

Both Petty Officer Allen and Petty Officer Robbins earned their warfare qualifications. But Petty Officer Robbins earned a second warfare qualification. This doesn't make Petty Officer Allen a less-than-stellar petty officer; he may have been at a command where it wasn't possible to earn a second warfare qualification. But if you have the opportunity to earn another warfare device, take it.

I earned the surface warfare qualification as a third class petty officer, well before it became mandatory. Then, while I was assigned as the senior enlisted leader at Mobile Security Squadron Two, the Expeditionary Warfare Qualification was approved, and I was able to earn that device as well.

Special Qualifications

You should also pursue special qualifications within your community or rating. These include qualifying as a command duty officer, which at most shore commands is a qualification open to first class petty officers and above.

The Master Training Specialist (MTS) qualification deserves special note. If you serve as an instructor for your rate's "A" school, you may have the opportunity to earn this qualification. There is a time requirement, so if you're there for less than a year and don't earn the qualification, it won't have a negative impact. However, if you're about to transfer after being an instructor for three years yet haven't earned your MTS qualification, it means you had the opportunity to achieve this goal but failed to do so. The chief petty officer selection board will certainly take notice, and this could be the reason you don't get selected. Failure to take advantage of such opportunities tells the selection board you're not ready to assume greater responsibility.

Watch Qualifications

You'll be required to achieve certain watch qualifications for your rating, and you need to pay attention to these. But since all of your peers will achieve them as well, focus on qualifications that will break you out from among your peers.

If you're a first class petty officer now assigned to shore duty, the command duty officer qualification may benefit you. Of course, this qualification may be required by the command. But even if so, you may be able to break out by serving as the watch bill coordinator. This will allow you to showcase your ability to stand the watch and exercise the responsibility of ensuring that the watch is stood by qualified personnel, both enlisted and officer.

If you're a first class petty officer assigned to a submarine, have done well on your watch qualifications, and have otherwise shown your readiness to take on more responsibility, maybe your chiefs will decide you're ready to qualify as a diving officer of the watch. This is a significant qualification, so you may not be allowed to fill this role. But it would certainly break you out from among your peers; if you got the opportunity, would you accept the challenge?

Perhaps you're a first class petty officer assigned to a surface combatant ship, a member of the Engineering Department. If given the opportunity to qualify as an engineering officer of the watch, would you accept the challenge?

No matter what community you're in, if opportunities like the last two examples came your way, would you step up to the challenge or just sit back and let some other first class petty officer seize it instead? Go back and read in the Preface what I said about doing the right thing for the right reason, and ignoring those who try to hold you back by pulling you down. Any opportunity you pass up may turn out to be the one that would have made the difference between being selected as a chief petty officer or watching some other professional pass you by.

Chapter 14

Sustained Superior Performance

Consistency

What does "sustained superior performance" actually mean? It means doing all the things expected of you every day—and more. This will help make you a well-rounded sailor, which will make you more competitive among your peers.

The key to maintaining sustained superior performance is consistency. To keep you competitive among your peers, maintaining this for only one or two years is not enough: you'll keep up, but only for a while. Sustained superior performance means going beyond the normal call of duty day in and day out, year after year. If this describes you, you're well on your way to becoming a chief petty officer; if it doesn't, you need to keep your goals in sight or they'll sail over the horizon without you.

Leading Petty Officer

One of the key factors the chief petty officer selection board will look at is your ability to lead sailors.

Are you a leading petty officer at sea? Have you ever had the opportunity? This constitutes one of the best opportunities to demonstrate to the selection board that you can lead sailors. If you haven't been a leading petty officer at sea, have you been one ashore? This is the next best opportunity to show the selection board you can lead sailors. If you haven't had the opportunity to be a leading petty officer of either kind, why not?

If you've never been given the opportunity to be a leading petty officer, don't be discouraged; it doesn't mean you won't be a chief petty officer. I was never given the opportunity to be a leading petty officer at sea or ashore. I applied myself to the other areas of the Wheel of Success, allowing me to shine elsewhere instead. But if you're given the opportunity to be a leading petty officer, grab it, and use it to show your ability to lead sailors. If you don't, you may never get another chance.

Sustained Superior Performance and Evaluations

Even if you're not a leading petty officer, you can still maintain sustained superior performance. When evaluations are conducted every year, are you consistently above the reporting senior's average? This is vital for you to be competitive, not only compared to your peers at your command but Navy-wide. Failure to be evaluated above the reporting senior's average sends the negative message to the chief petty officer selection board that you're not maintaining sustained superior performance.

The only exception to this guideline would be the first evaluation you receive at a new command, when you did not have a full year to compete among your peers. You still don't want to receive an evaluation below the reporting senior's average, but if this happens, what's important is to show upward mobility for the remaining years at the command. So, even if on your first evaluation at a new command you fall below the reporting senior's average, don't concern yourself about it; just consistently perform above and beyond your peers, and you'll be rewarded on your evaluations for your outstanding performance.

To constitute sustained superior performance, you must continue at a high level in each evaluation cycle. Getting a "must promote" evaluation for one cycle doesn't guarantee you'll receive an "early promote" evaluation the next time. There's nothing to say that the command won't give you a "promotable" evaluation for this cycle even if you received a "must promote" last cycle—the command is only required to give you what you earned. During any single evaluation cycle, other first class petty officers may outperform you, according to the evaluation ranking boards. If you don't sustain a superior performance, you decrease your chances of being competitive among your peers and of being selected as a chief petty officer. Conversely, maintaining and sustaining superior performance during each evaluation cycle will increase your chances of getting better evaluations and of being selected.

Are you a one-of-one for your annual evaluation? Although being ranked among your peers is best, sometimes being one-of-one is unavoidable. If you're in this situation, you must illustrate your capacity to take on additional command collateral duties, community involvement, education, and other areas that will showcase your ability to excel. If you are assigned other duties, make sure they're acknowledged in your evaluations; otherwise it's like not having performed them at all.

Robbins and Allen

Both of these petty officers were ranked very high within their commands. However, a closer look at the entire evaluations shows that Petty Officer Allen had collateral duties listed in block 29 but nothing written about them in block 43. Any additional duties you take on must be reflected in your evaluations. (See the previous discussion in Chapter 3.)

For example, Petty Officer Allen was the president of the First Class Petty Officer Association, but the lack of a write-up in block 43 indicates he did nothing other than "check a box" on his evaluation. In contrast, Petty Officer Robbins' evaluation in block

29 and his write-up in block 43 provide substantial information about his additional duties.

If you fail to use your evaluation to substantiate your qualifications, education, collateral duties, command involvement, or other areas of achievement, the chief petty officer selection board will never know about your achievements. If all you do is put a check in the box, it's like telling the selection board you did nothing at all.

Sustained Superior Performance and Goal-Setting

No matter what your goals are, achieving them gives you a sense of satisfaction that will usually give you the drive to set new goals. The success or failure of this continuing process of setting (and, we hope, achieving) goals establishes the tone for how effective or ineffective your career will be. Some sailors succeed at becoming chief petty officers without consciously setting goals, but if you do set and achieve goals it's likely to lead you down a successful path.

More frequently, sailors who don't set and achieve goals find other sailors passing them by in their careers. Do you know sailors you once worked for who now work for you? This is usually not a result of their bad luck but rather your hard work. However, if you're the sailor being passed by, I recommend you set some new goals, speak to your chief, and have a career development board. You may not be a bad sailor, or an unsuccessful one—but you need to get back on track.

Remember: you must be competitive with your peers! If you're not in the game you won't be selected. Take advantage of every opportunity; don't pass up a challenge! If, as a result, you get to excel and showcase your ability as a leader, your chiefs' mess will take notice, and the chief petty officer selection board likely will as well.

Chapter 15

Proven Deckplate Leadership

Deckplate Leadership and the Wheel of Success

Proven deckplate leadership is the sum of all the other parts of the Wheel of Success. Your overall involvement in all the areas of the Wheel will demonstrate your overall leadership attributes and potential as a sailor. Maximizing your proven leadership is the best way to showcase your talents to the chief petty officer selection board. Just as there is no one correct way to lead sailors, you must be able to demonstrate to the board the many facets of your ability to lead sailors. Being a deckplate leader means doing all the things that are expected every day—such as education, community service, command involvement, and all the other functions that make you a well-rounded sailor—and doing them well. A deckplate leader doesn't just participate in these activities, he or she takes charge and leads the way so others will follow. Being this kind of well-rounded sailor will make you more competitive among your peers, which will set you up for success down the road.

Each of the ten areas of the Wheel of Success has its own breakdown, with applicable points. There are no shortcuts to becoming a deckplate leader, but by using the Wheel you should be able to amass the maximum number of points within each area. This is not a short-term goal by any means, because it will take most sailors two to five years to achieve the maximum. Some sailors will be able to max out some of the areas quicker—education, for example, because they may already have earned a degree. Maybe you're someone who's been able to achieve points more quickly because of goals you've already set and achieved. But don't slow down! You may be ahead of some of your contemporaries in some areas, but likely not in others.

When you achieve a maximum score in each of the first nine areas, the Wheel awards you an additional ten points for deckplate leadership. The scores you achieve in each section determine your overall score. If you haven't received the maximum points in each section, add all of the points from the nine areas together, calculate an average per area, and add it to the subtotal to yield your total score. (For example, if your other scores total 63, divide by 9 to get 7.0 for deckplate leadership, and add them together for an overall score of 70.0.) This will give you a better picture of where you may stand among your peers. The higher your overall score, the more you showcase your ability to perform at a higher level—and that's better than just doing your job well.

A Final Note

At this point, as you look at the Wheel of Success, you should have a much better understanding of how it relates to setting and achieving the goals that will help you become a chief petty officer. My goal in writing this book and introducing you to the Wheel was to set you up for success.

Of course, the rest is up to you. You can take your career seriously and be a leader whom others will gladly follow, or you can just sit back and hope for the best—it's your decision. But I urge you to use every tool to your advantage. So, for the last time, my recommendation is: go to the chiefs' mess for guidance and direction!

How the Wheel of Success Works

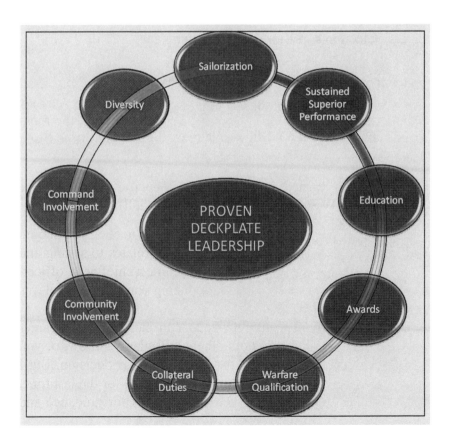

Although each discussion of a Wheel section below includes a percentage breakdown, it is only a guideline. Consult your chief for more information.

Awards (maximum 10 points)

☐ Personal awards received in career previous to current assignment (not counting IA awards or MOVSM)

- FLOC = 1% each; maximum 2%

- NAM = 2% each; maximum 8%

- NCM = 4% each; maximum 12%

  22% (2.2 points): achievable overall grade for this section

☐ Selection as Sailor of the Quarter/Year

- SSOQ = 2% for each selection; maximum of 6%

- SOY = 20% of grade

  26% (2.6 points): achievable overall grade for this section

☐ Awards earned during current tour (not including IA awards, MOVSM, or awards projected for end of current tour)

- If NAM or above, add 5%

  5% (.5 points): achievable overall grade for this section

☐ Awards for IA assignments

- NAM or equivalent = 8%

- NCM or equivalent = 10%

- Above NCM or equivalent = 20%

38% (3.8 points): achievable overall grade for this section

☐ Military Outstanding Volunteer Service Medal

9% (.9 points): achievable overall grade for this section

Collateral Duties (maximum 10 points)

Below are examples. All command and departmental collateral duties must show command impact. Command collateral duties carry more points than similar departmental collateral duties. It's possible to earn 10 points with only one command collateral duty, depending on the significance it has within the command.

Command Collateral Duties

☐ Command Fitness Leader (CFL) (max 10%)
☐ Urinalysis Program Coordinator (UPC) (max 10%)
☐ Drug and Alcohol Program Coordinator (DAPA) (max 10%)
☐ Mentorship Coordinator (max 10%)
☐ Command Career Counselor (max 10%)
☐ Diversity Committee Coordinator (max 10%)
☐ Command Management Equal Opportunity Coordinator (CMEO) (max 10%)
☐ Command Assessment Team (CAT) (max 10%)
☐ Command Training Team (CTT) (max 10%)
☐ Mess Decks Master-at-Arms (max 10%)
☐ Command Sponsorship Coordinator (max 10%)
☐ Funeral Honors Detail (max 10%)
☐ Departmental Collateral Duties
☐ Departmental Command Fitness Leader (max 3%)
☐ Departmental Urinalysis Coordinator (max 3%)

☐ Departmental Mentorship Coordinator (max 3%)
☐ Departmental Command Career Counselor (max 3%)
☐ Damage Control Petty Officer (max 3%)
☐ Engineering Department Log Room Yeoman
☐ Weapons Department Log Room Yeoman

10 points: achievable overall grade

Note: Don't overload yourself with too many collateral duties. If you're occupied throughout the day with collateral duties, you might be unable to lead.

Command Involvement (maximum 10 points)

☐ Office in the First Class Petty Officer Association (FCPOA)

- President = 20%

- Vice president = 15%

- All other positions = 10%

Note: to gain maximum points for an FCPOA position, you must be actively involved—just holding the title earns no points.

20% (2 points): achievable overall grade

☐ Positive impact within the command as a member of the FCPOA. Examples:
☐ Holiday food drives = 10%
☐ Clothing drives = 10%
☐ Command functions (command picnics, MWR events, Navy Ball fundraisers, etc.) = 10%
☐ Other = 10%

30% (3 points): achievable overall grade

☐ FCPOA-conducted advancement training (warfare qualification training, or specialized training such as DCTT, CSOOW, EOOW) in which you are involved
Conducted/involved = 20%

20% (2 points): achievable overall grade

Command Inspections (key role vs. participant)

☐ Inspection & Survey (INSURV) = 10%
☐ Joint Staff Integrated Vulnerability Assessment (JSIVA) = 10%
☐ CNO Integrated Vulnerability Assessment (CNOIVA) = 10%
☐ Explosive Safety Inspection (ESI) = 10%
☐ Unit-Level Training (ULTRA) = 10%
☐ Final Evaluation Problem (FEP) = 10%
☐ Hurricane Exercise (HURREX) = 10%
☐ Ongoing Professional Practice Evaluation (OPPE) = 10%
☐ Aviation Certification (AVCERT) = 10%
☐ 5-Star Bachelor Housing Inspection = 10%
☐ Solid Curtain = 10%
☐ Tactical Readiness Evaluation (TRE) = 10%
☐ Operational Reactor Safeguard Exam (ORSE) = 10%
☐ Pre-Overseas Movement Certification (POMCERT) = 10%
☐ Nuclear Weapons Technical Inspection (NWTI) = 10%
☐ Supply Management Inspection (SMI) = 10%
☐ Conventional Ordnance Safety Review (COSR) = 10%

30% (3 points): achievable overall grade

Add all the above subsections; maximum overall points for this section = 10 points

Note: Some command involvement may be worth more points than others within your respective community.

Community Involvement (maximum of 10 points)

Participation is good, but a leadership position in community service is better.

☐ Leading people in community service

15% for each event; maximum of 30%

30% (3 points): achievable overall grade

☐ Volunteering for community service

5% for each event; maximum of 15%

15% (1.5 points): achievable overall grade

☐ Letters of appreciation received from community service organizations

10% for each; maximum of 20%

20% (2 points): achievable overall grade

☐ Military Outstanding Volunteer Service Medal

35% (3.5 points): achievable overall grade

Note: Earning an MOVSM sends a positive statement to the board that you have consistently volunteered your time to the community.

Add all the above subsections; maximum overall points for this section = 10 points

Diversity (maximum of 10 points)

Challenging assignments (sea and shore)

☐ Instructor duty = 15%
☐ Recruiting duty = 15%
☐ Recruit Division Commander = 15%
☐ Rating community impact (Detailer/ECM, etc.) = 15%
☐ Individual Augmentee (IA)/Global Support Assignment

   (GSA)/Overseas Support Assignment (OSA) = 15%

   30% (3 points): achievable overall grade

Challenging assignments at your current command

☐ Productive IA/GSA/OSA = 15% each; maximum of 30%

   30% (3 points): achievable overall grade

Diverse sea/shore rotation. Examples:

☐ DDG = 20%
☐ CVN = 20%
☐ OCONUS = 20%
☐ LHA = 20%
☐ Independent duty = 20%

   40% (4 points): achievable overall grade

   Add all the above subsections; maximum overall points for this section = 10 points

Education (maximum 10 points)

☐ Pass the CPO test, become board-eligible
Earn/complete any of the following:

☐ CLEP, DANTES, college courses
= 1% each; maximum of 5% (.5 points)
☐ Associate's degree = 12% (1.2 points)
☐ Bachelor's degree = 22% (2.2 points)
☐ Master's degree = 31% (3.1 points)
☐ United States Military Apprenticeship Program (USMAP) = 12% (1.2 points)
☐ Military "C" school(s) (that will break you out in your rating) = 2% for each; maximum of 8% (.8 points)
☐ Navy correspondence courses (you should do at least one a year) = 1% for each; maximum of 5% (.5 points)
☐ Navy Knowledge Online (NKO) courses (not including mandatory rate or annual GMT courses) = 1% for each; maximum of 5% (.5 points)

Add all the above subsections; maximum overall points for this section = 10 points

Note: Some educational achievements may be worth more points within your respective community.

Earning multiple degrees of the same level (e.g., two associate's or two bachelor's degrees) gains you NO extra points for purposes of this section; however, it could gain you more points at the chief petty officer selection board.

Sailorization (maximum of 10 points)

Show positive retention of sailors you lead. Examples:

☐ Reenlistments & SRBs
= 3% for each sailor; maximum of 15%
☐ Awards (JSOQ/BJOQ, FLOC, MOVSM, NAM, etc.)
= 3% for each sailor selected as JSOQ/BJOQ; maximum of 15%

= 3% for each sailor who earns an MOVSM/NAM; maximum of 15%

45% (4.5 points): achievable overall grade

Sailors show signs of upward mobility. Examples:

☐ Advancement exams
Your sailors advance in rate
= 2% for each; maximum of 10%
☐ You provide mentorship and a positive role model for sailors, leading by example
= 5% for each protégé; maximum of 15%
☐ Education degrees your sailors earn through college, USMAP, and correspondence courses

5% for each degree earned/USMAP completed; maximum of 20%

1% for each correspondence course completed; maximum of 10%

55% (5.5 points): achievable overall grade

Add all the above subsections; maximum overall points for this section = 10 points

Warfare/Special/Watch Qualifications
(maximum 10 points)

If you are attached to a command that has warfare qualifications, you are required to qualify. Not receiving a warfare qualification will have a negative effect at the board.

☐ Warfare qualification completed (e.g., SW, AW, SS, SCW, EXW, FMF) = 10%
☐ Dual warfare qualifications earned (if assigned to a command where it is possible) = 10%

☐ NAC/MTS = 10%

30% (3 points): achievable overall grade

Watch Qualifications

Special qualifications earned while assigned to a duty station. Examples:

Aviation Community

☐ Command duty officer = 60% (shore duty only)
☐ Watchbill coordinator = 40%

Surface Navy

☐ EOOW = 80%
☐ CSOOW = 80%
☐ Command duty officer = 60% (shore duty only)
☐ Watchbill coordinator = 40%

Submarine Community

☐ Engineering Watch Supervisor (EWS) = 80%
☐ Chief of the Watch = 80%
☐ Diving Officer of the Watch (DOOW) =80%

Seabee Community

☐ Tactical supervisor = 80%
☐ Platoon commander = 80%
☐ Squad leader = 40%
   80% (8 points): achievable overall grade

Add all the above subsections; maximum overall points for this section = 10 points

Note: Other watch qualifications not listed above may be worth as many points, depending on the community and rating. You may receive higher points for qualifications within your rating than for those listed. Each community is unique within the Navy. For example, submariners deploy for months at a time, so may not have the opportunity to perform volunteer service; therefore, watchstanding duties may be worth more at the chief selection board. This doesn't mean submariners shouldn't strive for volunteer service, but their schedule makes the commitment difficult.

Sustained Superior Performance (maximum 10 points)

Evaluations

☐ LPO on sea duty = 25%
☐ LPO on shore duty = 15%
☐ Consistently above reporting senior's average = 2% for each year; maximum of 8%
☐ Breakout among peers = 10%
☐ Promotion recommendation. Working at the level of a chief, and reflected in your write-up: every time, sometimes, or not at all

Consistently yes = 10%

☐ Trend in evaluations: declining, consistent, or improving

Increase each eval cycle with the senior rater = 2% each; maximum of 6%

☐ One-of-one or versus peer group. (It's difficult to prove to the board that you have leadership qualities if you are consistently ranked one-of-one.)

Competitive among your peers, consistently year after year = 2% each year; maximum of 6%

80% (8.0 points): achievable overall grade

Description of Duties

☐ Position has impact on command mission, which is clearly reflected in your evals

2% each; maximum of 10%

☐ Increased responsibilities, reflected in your evals
5%

☐ Command/departmental collateral duties, reflected in your evals

5%

20% (2 points): achievable overall grade

Add all the above subsections; maximum overall points for this section = 10 points

Proven Deckplate Leadership (maximum 10 points)

Earning up to 10 points for each category re-listed below earns you up to 10 points for Proven Deckplate Leadership, making a possible grand total of 100 points. Your overall score is determined by the scores you've achieved in each section.

- If you achieve a maximum score in each of the nine areas, you receive the full additional 10 points for Deckplate Leadership (90 points + 10 points = 100).

- If you have not received the maximum points in each of the nine sections, add all of the points together, divide by

9 to get an average per section, and add the result to your subtotal to yield your total score. Example: if your overall score from the nine different categories subtotals 63, add 7.0 for Deckplate Leadership, giving you a total score of 70.0.

- ☐ Awards
- ☐ Collateral Duties
- ☐ Command Involvement
- ☐ Community Involvement
- ☐ Diversity
- ☐ Education
- ☐ Sailorization
- ☐ Sustained Superior Performance
- ☐ Warfare Qualification(s)

Proven Deckplate Leadership should take two to five years to achieve. Once you've attained this, you should continue to improve in each of the areas. It's important to continually update your goals as you achieve them. Achieving goals gives you a sense of satisfaction. So set short-term as well as long-term goals, and make sure they're achievable.

Don't set yourself up for failure instead of success. For instance, conditions may make it difficult to achieve a certain goal (e.g., you find you're unable to pursue your degree because deployment means limited time availability, poor continuity with the instructor, and no access to the internet). In such a situation, don't keep banging your head against the wall, only to become discouraged. Instead, put this goal on hold until you can get back to it, and turn to a different goal to achieve.

Results Between YN1 Robbins and YN1 Allen

YN1 Robbins	YN1 Allen	Awards
1.00	0.60	Personal awards (NCM, NAM, FLOC)
2.20	0.00	SOY/SOQ
0.50	0.00	EOT awards (NCM, NAM, FLOC)
2.00	0.00	IA, GSA, OSA
0.90	0.00	MOVSM
6.60	**0.60**	**Total for section**
	Collateral Duties	
10.00	5.00	Command
0.00	0.00	Departmental
10.00	**5.00**	**Total for section**

Command Involvement		
2.00	0.00	FCPOA president, vice president, treasurer, secretary
3.00	0.00	Positive impact as FCPOA within command
2.00	1.00	Provide advancement training, etc.
1.00	3.00	Command inspections
8.00	**4.00**	**Total for section**
Community Involvement		
3.00	0.00	Leading community involvement
1.50	0.00	Volunteering for community involvement
2.00	0.00	Letters of appreciation for community involvement
3.50	0.00	Military Outstanding Volunteer Service Medal
10.00	**0.00**	**Total for section**
Diversity		
1.50	1.50	Challenging assignments
3.00	0.00	Productive IA/GSA/OSA
2.00	2.00	Diverse sea/shore rotation
6.50	**3.50**	**Total for section**

Education		
0.20	0.00	College courses, CLEP, DANTES
1.20	0.00	Associate's degree
2.20	0.00	Bachelor's degree
0.00	0.00	Master's degree
0.00	1.20	USMAPS
0.20	0.40	Correspondence courses (outside career field)
0.40	0.30	NKO courses (outside career field)
4.20	**1.90**	**Total for section**
Sailorization		
0.00	1.50	Retention
1.20	0.00	Awards for your sailors
1.00	1.00	Upward mobility for your sailors
1.50	1.00	Provide mentorship
1.00	0.00	Education for your sailors
4.70	**3.50**	**Total for section**
Warfare Qualifications		
1.00	1.00	Earning a warfare qualification
1.00	0.00	Earning a dual warfare qualification
0.00	0.00	Special qualifications

Warfare Qualifications, continued		
8.00	8.00	Watch qualifications
10.00	**9.00**	**Total for section**
Sustained Superior Performance		
2.50	2.50	LPO sea duty
1.50	0.00	LPO Shore Duty
1.00	1.00	Evaluation breakout
1.00	0.50	Promotion recommendation
0.60	0.60	Consistently increase each eval cycle
0.60	0.40	Consistently ranked above peers
1.00	1.00	Description of duties at command reflected in evals
0.50	0.50	Increased responsibilities at command reflected in evals
0.50	0.20	Collateral duties reflected in evals
9.20	**6.70**	**Total for section**
69.20	**34.20**	**Subtotals for 9 sections**
7.69	3.8	Proven Deckplate Leadership
76.89	**38.0**	**Overall Score**

Deckplate Leaders

Those who have been entrusted as a chief petty officer will understand the information below because you have lived it. Those Sailors who are still goal-oriented and have set their sights on becoming a Chief, I want you to understand what I am about to say because everything you work for will be lost if you fail to establish credibility. That's right, credibility.

Being a senior enlisted leader in today's fast paced Navy is often predicated on establishing credibility. This is something that speaks volumes about oneself. Credibility is not something you achieve through the ranks. Credibility must be earned. The moment one's credibility is lost is the moment you lose the ability to be a leader. Sailors want to be led, they like to follow a good leader. But a leader doesn't mean you bark orders and move on. A leader is one whom others aspire to be like. Once you establish that, don't screw it up. If you do, it's almost impossible to earn it back.

Chief petty officers are Deckplate leaders. This is one of the primary reasons why the Chief's Mess is vital to the mission readiness of the Navy. Now I'm not saying that all of them are, because we have all seen that chief out there who gives the Mess a bad name. They are all about the rank, but not about the job. They are interested in what's best for them and not the Sailor. They are not a team player. The Mess refers to someone like this as an E7. I believe that covers that personality type, so let's move on.

Chief petty officers by and large have the experience and technical expertise to lead a group of Sailors with relative ease. This is a skill that requires a lot of dedication and preparation—not something achieved overnight. A Sailor feels a sense of comfort when they see their chief alongside them teaching and mentoring. They feel like they matter. This is because the Sailor does matter. In the eyes of the Chief, everyone matters or no one does. This includes the one or two Sailors in the division who are considered the problem children—the ones who often get into trouble. Although they may require a little more time from the chief, he or she will work to get them back on the right track. Sometimes it works, sometimes it doesn't, but the chief isn't going to give up without at least trying. In the end, some Sailors just aren't cut out to be in the Navy.

I saw this first hand when I was stationed aboard the USS *Monterey* (CG 61). I was a third class petty officer at the time. We had a second class petty officer who would just do his job. He was very bright, but didn't seem motivated by anything he was tasked with doing. He would do the job and do it well, but it seemed like he wasn't performing at his potential.

The leading chief petty officer took notice and pulled him to the side one day after quarters. The next day, he was my new work center supervisor. The division couldn't believe the chief had just taken an average working sailor and put him in charge of us. At first we were upset and didn't understand. Sometimes as Sailors you will see this and ask why?

It didn't take long for us to notice why the chief had done what he did. The second class petty officer pulled us all to the side after quarters the following day. He expressed to us what he expected of us. After he let this sink in a while, he asked us something I had never heard before. He asked what we expected of him. Just by asking those simple words he gained our trust.

I learned later the reason the chief did what he did was he discovered the second class petty officer hadn't been challenged enough. The chief seized the opportunity, even when this second class expressed his objections to the new position. The objections were duly noted, but the chief pressed on. Come to find out our new work center supervisor was not just a good technician, it turned out he was also a good leader.

Not only did the chief do what he thought was best for the division; I believe it enhanced his credibility with the department. He sent a clear message that the chief cares. He had the insight, knowledge, and experience to trust that young Sailor to lead us. It was a learning experience I never forgot.

The majority of a chief petty officers time may be spent in meetings. This is a fact of life in the Navy. That's why it's imperative that the chief is visible and instrumental in the development of each of his or her Sailors. The chief must be seen, not heard. Visibility breeds trust among your Sailors. Remember, a chief leads by example. This is through actions, not words.

I believe the biggest challenge future chief petty officers will face is the need to do more with less. The mission always comes first. This isn't going to change. This means future leaders in the Mess will be challenged to get the job done. This doesn't mean the chief will roll up their sleeves and get out there on the deckplates and fix the problem themselves. It means as leaders, the chief must be able to train those they lead. I'm not saying there won't be a time when the chief will have to roll up their sleeves and do some elbow grease, but by and far, as a leader; the chief must be able to lead. That's their job.

Chief petty officers must continue to lead from the front. In order for this to happen, senior enlisted leadership must remain acute to what motivates their Sailors. They must continue to understand how to leverage their numerous talents to contribute to mission-readiness.

Highly effective leadership is essential in the overall success of the Navy. The United States Navy has been blessed with top-notch chief petty officers. These senior enlisted leaders have been the fulcrum to the world's most dominating Navy for more than a century. They are the lynchpin that functions between the enlisted and officer community. You pull the pin and these elements no longer function together as a unit.

As the Navy changes in response to the ever-changing environment, the leadership must remain flexible and willing to lead different personalities. These often include but are not limited to leading different generational and cultural personalities through extremely adverse conditions.

As future chief's you must be willing to adapt to these changes. You will be tasked to ensure the core and structure of the command remains focused on the mission and vision of the Navy.

The Role of the Chiefs

As the military changes in response to the ever changing environment, leadership must remain flexible. They must be willing to lead different personalities and often times different generational mentalities through extremely adverse conditions. The Navy has groomed the chief petty officer to fulfill this arduous duty in a wide variety of ways.

As chiefs move up the ladder and become the future senior chiefs and master chiefs of the navy, they become highly skilled in leading and displaying leadership skills that are quite unique and valuable. The chief petty officer becomes the consummate professional. Their leadership traits allow them to lead their sailors up, down, and laterally. After all, being a chief is not a one dimensional job. They are the quintessential multitasker.

The chief resembles your mother or father growing up at home. And just like mom and dad are the common thread to any household, the chief petty officer is the common thread to any naval command. They have lived it, seen it, slept it and, most importantly, learned from past successes and failures.

Being able to learn from both past successes and failures is invaluable and part of the career progression of a chief petty officer. It's essential and even vital in the growth and development of the talented pool within the chief petty officer community. This is how future leaders in the Navy are groomed for success, not failure.

The United States Navy has always recognized the unique power and capability of the senior enlisted community. Although the chief petty officer is the first rung of the ladder in the senior enlisted community, this in no means states they are the least sought after by the enlisted sailors. In fact, if you look at each command, it is the Chief that most sailors will come to when they have a problem. Why is that?

Simply but, the Chief is the backbone of the Navy. It's been this way since 1893. It's not only the junior Sailors who seek the Chief's advice; the Wardroom also seeks the advice of the Chief petty officer. Why is this?

Well, for starters, it's the chief petty officer who is charged with training junior officers. I'm not saying that the Chief, the lowest rung on the ladder of the senior enlisted community, is the only one charged with this duty, but they are the ones who provide it the most.

"Ask the Chief." It's a phrase that's been used in the Navy by enlisted and officer alike over the years. It's what keeps our Navy moving forward. Although the Chief may not run the Navy, they definitely drive it.

The Chief is like the cog in a chronometer. Although there are many different parts to the timepiece, his role is to keep the clock moving forward. He's part of a team. A team that is vital to the overall success of the chronometer. The Chief is integral to the success of Navy operations. If you remove the cog, you remove all hope that the timepiece will continue to function in the precise manner in which it was designed. Simply put—the timepiece fails to function within specifications because the parts don't work together as a team.

Like the cog, the leadership of the Navy is dependent upon the Chief. The role they play is not an easy one. The path to becoming a Chief is also a difficult road to travel. In order to fulfill this role, you must be willing to make sacrifices to achieve this goal. I can attest to this as well as my many brothers and sisters who have filled the shoes as a chief petty officer before me as well as after I retired. The role of a Chief petty officer requires time management, leadership qualities, mentoring, and a cocktail mixture of ingredients needed to fulfill the job.

Now this may seem like it might be a little overpowering. A little more than one person can bear on their shoulders. Well, you would be correct. One Chief cannot do all of these things and still function as a Sailor. Remember when I mentioned the Chief is the backbone of the Navy. Well, the Chiefs Mess is the body that houses it. The Chief does not walk the passageways on board a ship alone. They have a network of support called the Chiefs Mess. The Mess is everywhere. If the Chief has a question, and there will be a time when you will as a chief petty officer, you will go to your Mess. It's not a question of if they will find the answer; it's a matter of when. With a network as large as the Chief's Mess, it's only a matter of time before they find the answer. This is the part of the job in which it will require your time. Sometimes only a minute, sometimes it may require hours or even days. In order to be a chief petty officer, you must be willing to sacrifice your time. After all, being a Chief is not about you, it's about your Sailors.

If this is something you don't want to take on, then don't. Not every Sailor is cut out to be a Chief. Maybe you'd be better off in the Wardroom. This is not meant to be a derogatory remark. The Navy needs good officers, especially ones who were once among the enlisted ranks. Just don't forget to utilize the Chiefs Mess. The camaraderie, espirit de corps, and wealth of knowledge the Mess brings to the table can only enhance your success, not hinder it.

When I was a chief petty officer at Naval Air Station Brunswick, Maine, I had the pleasure of working with two of the best leaders in my naval career: Gary Hastings and John Lippolis. I mentioned these two back in Chapter 2: Are you a leader?

At the time I held two positions: one as the Deputy Security Officer, the other as the Leading Chief Petty Officer for the Security Department. One of the first jobs assigned to me was getting ready for the first Blue Angels's air show in several years. In fact, it was the first air show since before 9/11. Security needed to be beefed up. We expected more than 100,000 spectators a day for the three day event.

To help get ready for an event of this magnitude, we started preparing months in advance. We held weekly meetings with the FBI, NCIS, Port Authority, and a dozen other agencies. All told, I had approximately 350 people working security detail for the air show.

The first day of the event, we certainly had 100,000 spectators show up to watch the air show. My security personnel provided traffic control, parking, entrance onto the airfield, and conducted searches of personal belongings brought in bags and backpacks.

We were supposed to be fed by the galley, but things didn't work out like they were supposed to. In the end, only a few dozen got food, water, and a break. As the man in charge of security, I was livid to say the least. I spoke with the manager of the galley to get some box lunches prepared for my staff, but he informed me he had others who needed to be fed first. Instead of causing a scene in the galley, I took a deep breath and exited.

The Commanding Officer held a meeting in his conference room when the show was over and spectators began leaving. He wanted to discuss the good, the bad, and the ugly. Most of the department heads spoke of the amount of revenue the air show brought in. Food, drinks, memorabilia, and other money making merchandise.

When it came my turn to share it was time to put up or shut up. I thought how John and Gary took a chance with me. They put me in charge of the security operations for the air show. They knew I had the knowledge, but did I have the courage to speak up for my people if things went wrong?

I chose to make a stand. I began with the lack of food my staff received. Next, I mentioned the few who received water got it from a water hose. I finished with the lack of support from the members at the table to give my personnel breaks.

The Commanding Officer was appalled upon hearing this. I gave a rundown of what I expected, then calmly excused myself from the room and went back out to help with traffic control.

The next two days, the department heads personally delivered boxed lunches to every security person on the base. They made so many of them, most of my personnel received two. In the end I decided to stand up and make sure my personnel were taken care of. With the support of the Commanding Officer and some elbow grease it got done.

So when you're a chief petty officer and a problem presents itself to you, what will you do? Will you take the challenge head on, sound the collision alarm to avoid it, or simply ignore it altogether? The choice will be yours to make. What will it be?

An Interview with Author James C. Glass, MACS, USN, Ret.

SB: Why did you decide to write this book?

JG: This book is a tool to help you achieve your goal of becoming a Chief Petty Officer. As a Sailor, there are many precepts you can use to guide yourself as you work your way to achieve your goal of becoming a Chief Petty Officer, but none are as specific as what you will find in *The Chief Petty Officer Guidebook*. I believe it's important to have specific information Sailors can obtain to set and achieve their goals. After all, setting and achieving goals are essential to your success; not just in the Navy but in any organization. In writing this book, it's my goal to help you achieve it.

SB: Why would someone want to become a Chief Petty Officer?

JG: The Chief is required to be a technical expert, a fountain of wisdom, and a leader for personnel under his or her charge. The satisfaction you receive knowing you've helped Sailors set and achieve their goals is just one of the shoes a Chief fills everyday.

SB: How did you prepare to become a Chief Petty Officer?

JG: In order to become a Chief in today's Navy, you must set realistic goals that will make you more competitive among your peers. One way to do this is to have a Career Development Board with your Chiefs. By doing both, I was able to achieve the rank of Chief. It's not an easy task, but at least you'll have a roadmap to guide you along the way, instead of driving blindly.

SB: What makes your book unique from other books on the same topic?

JG: Although there are several other books written about becoming a Chief Petty Officer, this is the first book written in detail and the most up-to-date. The book also compares two stellar First Class Petty Officers and how one set and achieved his goal of becoming a Chief Petty Officer, while the other did not.

SB: What are some features of your book that you think readers will really enjoy?

JG: The cornerstone of the book covers 'The Wheel of Success,' which breaks down ten distinct areas you should focus on to become more competitive among your peers. Being able to see these ten areas will help you focus on your goals. Once these goals have been identified, you will have a better chance of achieving them.

SB: What is a key take-away you want your readers to get from The Ultimate Chief Petty Officer Guidebook?

JG: Have you ever wondered what it takes to become a Chief Petty Officer in the United States Navy? There are no tricks or gimmicks which will get you to this level in the Navy. Becoming a Chief Petty Officer takes drive, initiative, and hard work.

Becoming a Chief Petty Officer is not just about rank. It's the pride you have knowing you can make a difference. Not only for the Sailors under your charge, but within the Navy as a whole. If you feel this is the path you want to take in your career, then you must read *The Ultimate Chief Petty Officer Guidebook.*

SB: Thank you.

JG: You're welcome.

Index

James Glass

James Glass achieved the rank of Command Master Chief before retiring after 22 years in the United States Navy. He is a graduate of the Senior Enlisted Academy and the Command Master Chief School. This is his first book. He was born in Pensacola, Florida, and enlisted in the Navy in 1989.

Author

He completed tours aboard the USS *Mobile Bay* (CG 53), USS *Yosemite* (AD 19), USS *Monterey* (CG 61), and USS *Thomas S. Gates* (CG 51). He also completed tours at Shore Intermediate Maintenance Activity, Mayport, Florida; Naval Air Station Brunswick, Maine; and Mobile Security Detachment Two-three in Portsmouth, Virginia. Finally, James completed two tours in Iraq during Operation Iraqi Freedom.

After retiring from the Navy, he and his family moved back to Florida. He's been married for 23 years and has two children. James and his wife welcomed their first grandson in November. James has a Bachelor of Science degree in Applied Management from Grand Canyon University.